AS Film Studies
UNIT 1

WITHDRAWN

WJEC

Unit FS1: Film — Making Meaning 1

Tanya Jones

Philip Allan Updates
Market Place
Deddington
Oxfordshire
OX15 0SE

Tel: 01869 338652
Fax: 01869 337590
e-mail: sales@philipallan.co.uk
www.philipallan.co.uk

© Philip Allan Updates 2003

ISBN-13: 978-0-86003-925-9
ISBN-10: 0-86003-925-0

This Guide has been written specifically to support students preparing for the WJEC Film Studies Unit 1 examination. The content has been neither approved nor endorsed by WJEC and remains the sole responsibility of the authors.

Printed by Raithby, Lawrence & Co. Ltd, Leicester

Environmental information
The paper on which this title is printed is sourced from managed, sustainable forests.

Contents

Introduction

■ ■ ■

Content Guidance

■ ■ ■

Coursework Samples

Introduction

About this guide

This guide is for students following the Welsh Joint Education Committee AS Film Studies course. It deals with **Unit FS1: Film — Making Meaning 1**. This coursework unit is designed to give you a good understanding of film form, the production of meaning and spectator response. There are three sections to this guide.

- **Introduction** — this section provides advice on how to use the guide, an explanation of the skills required for the unit, an outline of the tasks and guidance on study skills.
- **Content Guidance** — this section outlines the areas you will need to focus on for the unit. It is designed to help you get to grips with key concepts and terminology and offers suggestions for structuring your coursework pieces.
- **Coursework Samples** — this section provides exemplar contributions for all three parts of the unit coursework. It offers examples of grade-A and grade-C standard coursework. These are accompanied with commentaries which explain how the marks are awarded.

How to use the guide

To get the maximum possible benefit out of this guide, use it systematically. Make sure you read through the whole of the introduction carefully. When you have a thorough overview of the skills needed for this unit and the tasks you will be required to complete, you should move on to the next section.

The Content Guidance section aims to lead you through the essential content areas and highlight particular skills and theories. It would be extremely useful for you to make notes on your own examples and experiences as you read through the content areas. You have essential experience as a consumer of cinema, and the exam board encourages the addition of points that reflect your own experience.

When you have completed your study of content, you should then move on to look at the Coursework Samples section. Here you will find examples of types of course-work question. For each of the tasks, grade-A and grade-C answers have been provided, to illustrate what it takes to achieve a high grade. Take note of the struc-ture of the best answers, as well as the information they contain. Make sure that you read the accompanying comments on each answer, too, noting the features of the answers which are praised and the possible pitfalls.

The Unit 1 specification

This is the first unit of your AS Film Studies course. So that you are not introduced to an overwhelming amount of information at the beginning of the course, the unit aims to draw on your existing knowledge of films (Hollywood genre films in particular), while at the same time introducing you to a range of new concepts and terminology.

The three tasks which you will be asked to complete are a macro (wide) analysis of a film sequence (or two sequences), a micro (close) analysis of a film sequence, and a piece of practical work — either a storyboard or a screenplay.
- For your macro study, you will be asked to discuss how narrative and genre function in a particular film.
- For the micro study, you will be asked to analyse the use of the micro elements of *mise-en-scène*, cinematography, sound and editing.
- The storyboard and screenplay tasks require you to come up with an original idea for a film, create a storyboard or screenplay for a sequence of your choice and then write a synopsis, analysis and evaluation of your work.

The films that you study can be from American, British or another national cinema. The only stipulation is that these films are accessible and appealing to an audience. You should avoid choosing films that are too abstract, avant-garde or experimental.

Making Meaning 1 aims to give you a solid basis from which to further your film studies knowledge. It concentrates on how film form (the shape and structure of a film) works to generate meaning for the spectator and how the audience responds to the film form it is being offered. Your own experience as a consumer of film should be brought into your essays — personal reflection is encouraged by the examination board.

The unit aims to equip you with the terminology and conceptual understanding needed to become a more confident and challenging film analyst. The knowledge you gain of genre, narrative, *mise-en-scène*, cinematography, sound and editing will be applicable to your studies throughout the A-level course.

Skills required for the unit

The three main skills you will need to demonstrate in the Unit 1 are:
- an ability to show how the form and style of a film work to communicate meaning
- an ability to discuss how film form and style engage the audience
- an ability to reflect on and discuss your own experience as a consumer of film

In order to show your ability within the first of these skill areas, you will need to make sure that you understand clearly what the terms 'film form' and 'film style' mean. These terms are discussed at length in the Content Guidance section of this guide; however, for the purposes of clarity in this section, here is a brief definition of each term:

- **Film form** refers to the 'shape' of a film, how it is structured in terms of overall story and individual scenes.
- **Film style** refers to the particular way a film uses elements such as editing, sound or conventions of genre to create sense and meaning.

Your discussions of how a particular film generates meaning through its form may consider which storytelling techniques a film uses or how the individual scenes are organised. If your chosen film ends with a resolution, where all the pieces of the cinematic jigsaw are brought together, then you could comment on the impact of this type of explained ending on the cinema audience. You might discuss a voice-over used in your film and consider the impact on the viewer of having a narrative 'guide' to help navigate the way through a film. You might comment on the placing of seemingly unconnected scenes next to one another and consider whether the audience is being drawn into making some kind of conclusion about the events in the story through this organisation. Your discussions of a film's style might identify particular use of a **genre** element (choreographed action sequences in action films or frightening places in horror films, for example) and analyse what reaction the film is attempting to draw from its audience. You might look at a specific camera movement or camera angle used repeatedly in your film and offer your thoughts on how it positions the viewer in relation to the action being presented. You could consider how the use of sound in your chosen film is similar to or different from its use in other films of the same genre and discuss its impact on the viewer.

The second of the skills needed for this unit is the ability to discuss how film form and style engage an audience. You should translate 'engage' as the ways in which an audience is encouraged to respond. You are asked in the Unit 1 tasks to consider what kind of response the viewer might have to the macro and micro elements you have identified in your essays. You might discuss how the particular use of a camera angle might influence the viewer's identification with a character, or pick out a particular piece of music from the soundtrack and consider how it is used to create apprehension and fear in the audience. You might discuss the way in which two scenes have been edited together and speculate on how this might help the viewer to understand aspects of the plot.

The last of the skills identified in this section is the ability to reflect on and discuss your own experience as a film consumer. You will have a wide range of experiences to draw on and should select those that are most relevant to your macro and micro discussions. Consider how you reacted to camerawork, editing, sound, *mise-en-scène*, narrative and genre in the films you have chosen to study. You should discuss your reactions to these elements in similar films that you have seen outside the class-room.

The tasks

Unit 1 is worth 40% of your AS marks and 20% of the whole A-level grade. Within the unit, the tasks have individual value. Each of the two pieces of written analysis (macro and micro) is worth 30% of the unit total and the practical work is worth 40%.

The written pieces need to be between 1,000 and 1,500 words long — you should not exceed the upper word limit. Each piece is allotted 30 marks.

The **macro task** is either an analysis of one film or an analysis and comparison of two films. In either case, you should focus on how genre and narrative create meaning and generate a response in the viewer. If you choose just one film, you will need to select a sequence of no more than 10 minutes for your analysis; and if you choose to analyse sequences from two films, each sequence should be no longer than 5 minutes.

For the **micro study**, your task is to select one or more from the micro elements list (*mise-en-scène*, cinematography, sound and editing) and discuss how your chosen elements create meaning and generate an audience response. For the micro study you will analyse only one film, choosing a sequence of no more than 7 minutes.

For the practical (creative) work — an imaginary film — there are four length stipu-lations that you should remember. The **synopsis** of the film and the **account of cinematic ideas** (together worth 10 marks) should not exceed 200 words each. If you choose to complete a **screenplay extract** (shooting script), this needs to be between 500 and 800 words long. If you choose to do a **storyboard**, you should show between 15 and 25 shots. (This option, screenplay extract or storyboard, is worth 20 marks.) The last piece of writing to consider within your practical task is the **evaluation**, which should be between 400 and 500 words long (worth 10 marks). You should try to adhere to these word limits. However, pieces of writing that are up to 10% under or over these limits will be tolerated by examiners.

Your practical work is generated from an original idea. You will therefore need to focus on your own created film, rather than an industry example. Your synopsis will outline the key elements within the whole film, but the cinematic ideas will refer only to the sequence that you have chosen to make into a storyboard or screenplay. When presenting your plans for the cinematic ideas, you can refer to the elements of films which you think are similar to those you plan to use or which have been influential in creating your own original film. The evaluation section of this task asks that you reflect on your storyboard or screenplay and discuss its successful elements. It is not only your own assessment which is relevant here; you could ask members of your class for comments and add them to your evaluation.

Study skills

As with any AS course, it is essential that you organise your notes effectively. You probably will not have studied film before and it is, therefore, essential that any new content information, terms or concepts are recorded in your notes clearly and accurately. Make sure that you divide your notes into sections that relate to the tasks you will have to complete: macro analysis, micro analysis and practical work.

Macro analysis.

For the macro section of your notes, the two main terms to consider are **genre** and **narrative**. Under genre, begin by writing a clear definition of the term and then note down other key words that will be important for you to think about. You will need to refer to 'conventions' in your essay, for example, and so you should make sure that you include a clear definition of this term in your notes.

For each film genre, you need to know the key conventions and have examples of films. When discussing the function of genre in your coursework essays, you will need to show your understanding of how the film industry uses genre in the marketing of films and the expectations that an audience has of different genres, so your notes should include comment on these issues too.

Begin your notes on narrative with a general definition and then become more specific. There will be terms, such as 'equilibrium', 'disruption' and 'resolution', which will need further definition, backed up by examples from films. The impact of narrative devices on the film viewer (including yourself) will be an important area of discussion within your essay and you should note down the potential impact of, for example, resolved or unresolved storylines, disrupted equilibriums and narrative devices such as flashbacks.

Micro analysis

In the micro section of your notes, you should have clear definitions for the four elements you will need to choose from for your coursework essay: *mise-en-scène*, cinematography, sound and editing. Under each of these definition headings, it is useful to have subheadings which explain particular terms relevant to each of the micro elements. For example, for the micro element of editing, you should have a general definition of the term and the subheadings of other relevant terms, such as 'montage editing' and 'continuity editing', with your own specific definitions. The easiest way to learn terms and remember them is through reference to clear, cinematic examples.

Make sure you also make a note of the impact on the viewer (yourself included) that each of these elements of a film might have. These individual notes and examples will be invaluable when you come to choose your film for the analytical essay, as they will provide clear guidance on how to apply terminology accurately.

Practical work

The notes relevant to your practical work should be organised in the same systematic manner. Include industry examples of storyboards and screenplays, with notes about the key content and structural elements of each. Synopses of recently released films in film magazines can provide a useful reference for your own synopsis writing. Collect a few and note the kind of information and structure they share.

The terminology you will need within your notes on cinematic ideas can be drawn from your macro and micro notes, so you will not need to repeat definitions. It is useful, however, to record key ideas for sound, editing, cinematography and *mise-en-scène* which you have identified as successful or interesting in films you have seen. These references can be incorporated into your comments about your own screenplay or storyboard plans.

The unit has a dual function: it produces your first pieces of coursework and at the same time provides an essential building block for the rest of your course. If you define terms clearly in your notes and identify useful examples while working on this unit, you will have provided yourself with a glossary of terms and a store of film references which you can use throughout your AS and A-level Film Studies course.

Content
Guidance

This section summarises the main areas you need to focus on in your preparation for the unit tasks. It outlines content information, key issues and useful terminology and gives guidance on how to use your knowledge in your coursework pieces. The notes you have made in class and the information given to you by your teacher should be used alongside the information given in this section. Your personal investigations into the form and style of films, using your own observations or those from film textbooks, magazines, websites and other resources, should also be added to notes you take from this section.

This section covers:

- **Written analysis 1: the macro study** — including an outline of the task, key terminology definitions, and guidance on how to write your macro analysis.
- **Written analysis 2: the micro study** — including an outline of the task, key terminology definitions, and guidance on how to write your micro analysis.
- **Practical application of learning** — including task outlines, key features of story-boards and screenplays, and guidance on how to create the written sections.

Films that have an 18 certificate have been identified with an asterisk. The WJEC Film Studies AS specification allows the use of 18-certified films. However, if you choose an 18-certified film for your macro or micro study, you should discuss your choice with your teacher before commencing your written analysis.

Written analysis 1: the macro study

Your study of the macro elements of film will culminate in the production of an essay of between 1,000 and 1,500 words. This essay focuses on how narrative and genre create meaning and generate a response in the viewer. For this task you need to choose a sequence of no more than 10 minutes from one film as the focus for the study or two sequences of no more than 5 minutes each from different films. Any film you choose for this task should be relatively recent, have had mainstream cinema release and be easily accessible to you. You will find the task difficult if you pick obscure films, so choose a film you like and a sequence in which the macro elements are clearly defined.

The macro elements

For ease of understanding, the term **narrative** can be translated as story construction and movement. The term **genre** describes the group or category which your chosen film(s) falls into. Narrative and genre cannot be 'seen' within a film, as *mise-en-scène*, for example, might be. However, the choices a filmmaker makes regarding narrative and genre elements are equally important in the construction of meaning.

You do not need to use complex theories in order to discuss genre and narrative effectively, but you need to be aware of how they function. The remainder of this section aims to clarify each of the terms and give you an understanding of how the elements of each create meaning.

Genre

Genre is a French word, which literally means 'type'. Within film studies, genre is a word used to describe different categories or groups of films. There are many examples of genres of film, including Westerns, musicals, science fiction films, horror films and thrillers. Films within specific genres utilise similar elements: characters, story types, settings, costumes, props and themes.

Individual examples within a genre may use a particular resource in an unusual way. However, Westerns invariably include cowboys, sheriffs, saloons and saloon girls and horror films include frightening places, killers and victims.

Often, each main genre group can be subdivided into subgenres. For example, within the category of horror films, are the subgenres of vampire, slasher and demonic possession. Comedies can be romantic, slapstick and screwball. Don't forget that films may mix genres and become hybrid forms. A film could be classified as science fiction/horror, for example, or comedy/western. Your chosen film may be an example of one of these subgenres or hybrid forms and you should make sure that you identify clearly what you think it is.

In the film industry, genre provides some degree of predictability for producers. Each film produced is essentially different — in terms of cast, setting and story. If they were all the same, the audience would only ever have to see one film.

Each product of the film industry is a new investment — and this creates risk. Film producers are often drawn to films of a particular genre because they seem to lessen this risk. Genres begin with the box-office success of a particular type of film. Success results in the production of similar films, which resemble the first in plot (plot differs from story, in that a plot provides the structural shell for the film's story detail) and character types. Once a group of films of the same kind has been produced, a genre is born.

The success of the first example of the genre encourages producers to invest in other examples of that genre. The industry assumes that, if an audience was prepared to see the first film, similar films will be financially successful. Consider the spate of disaster films that hit the screens in the 1990s: *Armageddon*, *Deep Impact*, *Dante's Peak* and *Twister* followed one another in quick succession. Disaster films have always seemed to be popular. In the 1970s, audiences were offered *Airport*, *The Poseidon Adventure* and *The Towering Inferno* within a few years of one another.

Once a genre has proved itself to be a financial 'good bet' for producers, it can be recycled for any decade of viewers. 'Blockbuster' is a term often used to describe high-budget, special-effects-laden, huge-release Hollywood films with high production values and big returns at the box office. 'Blockbuster' films share certain characteristics and may provide an interesting example of a generic group in its own right.

For the film viewer, genre provides a means by which one type of film can be differentiated from other types; it provides a means of recognition. Viewers might choose to see a film because they enjoy a particular genre and want to experience predictable elements. Part of the group of expectations viewers have of a film text will be connected with their knowledge of the genre elements. However, there is an expectation that the elements will be used in a new and interesting way. Films that use generic conventions in an original way, playing with them or using them in a self-conscious fashion, keep the audience interested and sustain the popularity of the genre.

When you have chosen your film(s) for your macro study and are considering genre elements and their function, begin by asking yourself three questions:

(1) What are the generic conventions evident within the sequence or sequences I have chosen?

(2) How are these generic elements used in the sequence?

(3) What is the impact of their use on the audience?

Example

The opening sequence of Wes Craven's horror/slasher film *Scream** (1996)

(1) Generic conventions in the sequence

Narrative movement from safety to danger

Casey Becker (Drew Barrymore) feels safe in her family home and is about to begin a comfortable evening of video viewing. The situation quickly dissolves when the killer invades her safety and causes disruption and death.

Obscuring mise-en-scène

Horror films use darkness, mists, fog and other mechanisms to make the victim seem more vulnerable and the killer more threatening. Casey's bright house is thrown into darkness as she turns out the lights. The burning popcorn causes smoke, which impedes the viewer's and Casey's view. Both of these *mise-en-scène* elements work to disorientate and scare the character and the viewer.

Atmospheric use of diegetic and non-diegetic sound

From the opening credit sequence, we are presented with a mix of conventional horror sounds. The knife slash, slamming door and screams establish the horror genre. The ringing of a telephone is also associated with these introductory sounds and it becomes clear that the ringing of the phone introduces the killer into the victim's world. The sound of the smoke alarm as Casey is trapped in the house adds to the atmosphere of fear and panic. The non-diegetic horror sounds from the opening credit sequence, along with the diegetic sound of the increasing, threatening phone rings and alarm sounds, all add to the atmosphere of the sequence.

Represented groups

Slasher films are a subgenre of horror, which often use teenagers as the victim group. John Carpenter's *Halloween**, Wes Craven's *A Nightmare on Elm Street** and *Scream** all centre on a group of teenagers who are gradually 'picked off' by the killer. Casey Becker is, therefore, typical of the victim in a slasher film.

Iconography of knives and other 'body intrusive' weapons

Horror films can often be distinguished from action or thriller films because of the types of weapons used. The proximity of the killer is closer if a knife is used. The implication of a violent intrusion into the victim's personal space is heightened. Casey is attacked with a knife and her stabbing is graphically presented to the viewer.

The monster

The killers within horror films are often presented as monstrous. Their actions and motivations are incomprehensible to victims and audience alike. They are beyond the rational and comprehensible, thus becoming absolutely frightening because they will kill regardless of morality and reason. Killers in horror films might be monsters (Gothic horror — werewolves, vampires and mummies) or supernatural attackers (Freddy Krueger existed in dreams in the *Nightmare on Elm Street** series) or they might have incomprehensible psychologies (Michael Myers in *Halloween** or Norman Bates in *Psycho**). These killers are often masked in some way. Their identity is hidden by either a 'fake' personality or a mask. Casey Becker's killer in this sequence from *Scream** is relentless, unstoppable and his identity is hidden by a mask.

(2) Use of generic elements

The examples above list some of the uses of generic elements in this sequence. Wes Craven has established atmosphere, character type, narrative and the killer's 'persona' through the generic conventions used. However, Scream* is a different type of slasher film from its predecessors. It is an example of a self-conscious slasher film, by announcing its genre not only through its use of conventions, but also in the discussions that occur throughout the film. In this sequence, as Casey is about to settle down to watch a horror film, she has an initial conversation with the killer about horror film preferences. After she realises that the person at the other end of the phone is dangerous and is threatening her life, she is subjected to a quiz about horror film details. With both the dialogue and generic elements, Wes Craven signals to the viewers the genre of film they are watching.

(3) Impact on the audience

Horror films elicit a physical, as well as an emotional, response from the audience. The function of a horror film is to frighten the viewers, to make them uncomfortable, tense and fearful of what they will see next. This sequence from Scream*, through its use of generic elements, disorientates and scares the audience. It prompts a physical response.

The sequence establishes a pattern for the viewing of the rest of the film. The viewers understand that they are watching a horror film; this initial sequence presents almost a mini-version of the whole. The character feels safe, her environment is then invaded, she becomes more and more disorientated and trapped and eventually dies. The codes of character, place and action recognition are clearly established in this sequence. What is different about Scream*, and this sequence from it, is that it acknowledges its genre to the viewers and involves them in a 'discussion' of the slasher genre. They are asked to bring their own knowledge of horror films and their conventions into the viewing process. They use their own horror-viewing history to enter into the discussion about horror film preferences between Casey and the killer, and attempt to answer Casey's 'quiz' questions with her. The difference for the viewers with this type of film is that it not only provides the horror/slasher elements they expect, but also packages them in a knowing and acknowledged way. The audience is given the safety of met expectations, but also the interest value of a new presentation of the expected elements.

Your sequence(s)

Consider the film sequence(s) you have chosen in the ways described above. Which generic elements can you identify? How are they used? Are they used in any way that is different? If you can answer these three questions, you will provide a clear, thorough and original analysis of genre in your macro essay.

Having read through the whole of this section on genre, use the checklist of questions below to make sure that you have analysed genre in general terms and in your sequence specifically.

- How does genre help the film industry to minimise the risk of financial failure?

- What is the genre of my chosen film and what are the generic elements presented in the sequence?
- Are these generic elements used in a new or original way?
- What is the impact of the generic elements and their particular use on the audience?
- Why do genre films need to evolve and develop?

Key words

generic elements; subgenre; blockbuster; hybrid genre

Narrative

Narrative describes how stories are told to the viewer in terms of the structure and movement of a story within a film. You do not have to employ complex theories of narrative in order to provide a good analysis of its function. In any film, the settings, characters and events may be different, but there will be structural elements that are constant. Once you have decided on the sequence(s) for your macro essay, you will need to decide which of these structural elements are most relevant to your discussions.

On a very basic level, all films have the same narrative pattern. Stories move through the following stages: exposition, development, complication, climax, resolution.

Example

Steven Spielberg's *Minority Report* (2002)

Exposition
The exposition of a film's narrative introduces the setting and the characters to the viewer. *Minority Report* opens with scenes that introduce the futuristic setting, Tom Cruise's character (John Anderton) and the role of the Pre-Cogs.

Development
In the development section, the storyline is taken further and more characters are introduced. We are shown the workings of John Anderton's law enforcement organisation, his lost son, his ex-wife and the other characters who will have significance in the story.

Complication
During this stage of the film's narrative, we are presented with a complicating event which will affect the lives of the main characters. In *Minority Report*, the discovery of the possibility that the three Pre-Cogs might not always agree on their predictions for future crimes and that, in fact, there is a crime on which they did not agree provides the first part of the complication. The second complicating factor comes in the form of John Anderton's shift from law enforcement official to hunted perpetrator of a crime.

Climax
This is the point at which dramatic tension is at its height and we uncover the mystery of the story or have our questions answered. John Anderton's discovery of the truth about the lost 'minority report' provides the climactic section.

Resolution

The resolution sequence re-establishes stability and restores a form of calm. In the final scene, John Anderton is reunited with his now pregnant wife, looking forward to a new future.

Your sequence(s)

In order to delve deeper into the way in which the narrative elements of your sequence function, you could identify the 'forces' (characters, for example) at work which have an impact on the different sections outlined above, and you could consider whether your sequence has any unusual narrative features.

Perhaps your sequence provides the exposition. Usually, exposition sequences present the viewer with a situation that is calm, safe or at least predictable for the characters involved. You will need to identify not only what information is given in your exposition sequence, but *how* it is presented to the viewer. The setting might appear tranquil. It might create a positive mood through *mise-en-scène*. It might show characters involved in the day-to-day workings of normal life. The equilibrium (safe, calm, predictable situation) of your exposition scene can be created through dialogue, setting, *mise-en-scène* and sound elements.

Alternatively, you might choose a sequence that provides a development section. If so, you will need to consider how and why new characters are presented to the audience and what the impact is of new information given in this section. A new character who conflicts with the main character in some way (through an argument, for example) might be a disruptive force within the remainder of the film. Problematic information about the main protagonist given within the sequence might introduce a 'flaw' in the central character which will have an impact on later actions and events.

If your chosen sequence comes from the complication section of the film, you need to identify the central character's reaction to the complication, the role of any disruptive characters and the viewers' response to the complicating elements. You could discuss *how* the complicating factor is shown, whether it is within a parallel scene, showing the planning of the disruptive character, or introduced to the audience through a point-of-view shot, which allows the viewers to experience the complication as if they were the main character. Don't forget that camerawork and editing, along with *mise-en-scène* and sound, contribute to our understanding of narrative events.

If you have chosen part of the climax of the film, you need to identify the means by which the answers to the film's narrative questions are given. Does the protagonist have a revelatory conversation with another character? Is this a character whose previous position within the film has been one of trust? Are the answers given within an action sequence, in which the protagonist eventually kills the character who has provided the threat and complication within the story? Narrative 'answers' do not have to come in the form of information: events may halt the complicating factors.

Sequences from the resolution introduce a state of calm both to the characters and to the audience. The chaos and drama throughout much of the film are replaced by a new situation and a new kind of calm. The sequence may use *mise-en-scène* to present this calm. Maybe the colours and setting in which you find your characters at the end of the film are associated with safety and peace. You could discuss audience expectations of endings. If viewers are given resolution, they have a sense of their expectations having been met.

Narrative helps to organise groups of events into a pattern of cause and effect. We see an event and are then given information about its effect. The viewers see the consequences of actions that have occurred and feel that their expectations of the film's narrative have been met. If viewers were not shown the effect of a crime or a character's actions, they might feel cheated. They might be shown the consequences of an event through a close-up of a character's reactions, for example, or through a conversation between two characters.

One of the functions of narrative is to organise time and space. Within a 3-hour film, years of story may have been compressed, but the way in which the narrative is handled makes this compression of time invisible to the audience. If the narrative omitted significant events within a compressed time structure, the audience would question the sense of the film, and the artificiality of 'film time' would become more noticeable.

Look out for any points within the sequence you have chosen where there are leaps of time. How are they achieved? Why don't we need to see what happened in the time period that has been lost? The 'squashing' of time to fit a 2- to 3-hour period requires the viewers to take a leap of faith and trust that the film is giving them all the information they need. Within the type of film you choose for the macro study, you will probably not find any complex time structures, but you might well find time compression, which you will need to discuss.

Discuss any 'flashback' or 'flashforward' elements (narrative strategies that organise time) and try to identify their function. What information is given and what impact does that information have on characters and the audience? After reading this narrative section carefully, you should be able to write a detailed study of how narrative functions in your film sequence. Below is a checklist of questions to use in order to make sure that you have covered all relevant information.

- In which section of my film does the sequence come?
- What are the elements within my sequence which provide narrative information?
- How does my sequence organise time?
- How does my sequence show the effect of actions that occur?
- How do the narrative elements I have identified help viewer understanding?

Key words

position; development; complication; climax; resolution; equilibrium; disruption; flashback; flashforward; cause and effect

Writing your macro study essay

For this piece of coursework, you have 1,000–1,500 words in which to discuss how narrative and genre create meaning and generate response in either one film sequence of up to 10 minutes or two film sequences of up to 5 minutes. As with any piece of analytical writing, it is essential that you back up your points with clear textual detail. Before you begin writing, decide on what you think are the main issues concerning the functions of narrative and genre in your sequence. Once you have decided on these, you should work systematically through the sequence, highlighting examples that illustrate your points. Do not waste time telling the story of the sequence. Below are guidelines for organising your essay effectively.

The specification instruction is as follows:

> Focus on how narrative and genre features create meaning and generate response in a film sequence of no more than 10 minutes or in a comparison of two sequences from different films, neither of which should be more than 5 minutes in length.

Introduction

Introduce your essay by showing that you understand the terms **narrative** and **genre** clearly. You do not have to give definitions, but could state the main functions of both. Don't forget to discuss the function of genre and narrative for both the film audience and the producers of the film. For example, you could discuss the relationship between genre and audience expectations or highlight the role of narrative as a means by which time and space are organised in a film.

You need to state the film's title, director and date and identify the sequence you have chosen to study and its position within the film. Have you chosen an introductory sequence, an action sequence or a sequence that offers resolution?

The main body of your essay

In this section, you identify the features of narrative and genre that are evident in the sequence you have chosen. Make sure that you always refer to the impact on the audience which these identified features may have. You could split your paragraphs into two sections: one that deals with narrative and one that deals with genre. As you move through your analysis, discussing the features of narrative and genre, it is useful to keep the following questions in mind, as they will help you to identify the use of narrative and genre conventions within the sequence.

- To what extent does the sequence adhere to conventions? Does it subvert them or use them in an unusual way?
- Does the sequence 'play' with conventions in order to engage the audience?
- Is the film self-conscious in its use of conventions? Does it discuss its own conventions in a knowing way?

- Are any of the actors in your film associated with particular genre or narrative types? Does this affect the audience's response to the film?

Conclusion

Your conclusion should summarise the main points within your essay and include a comment on how effective the use of genre and narrative has been in the generation of meaning and engagement of the audience.

Written analysis 2: the micro study

Your study of the micro elements of film will eventually culminate in the production of a 1,000–1,500 word essay, which analyses how one or more of *mise-en-scène*, editing, sound and cinematography create meaning and generate a response in the audience. You have to choose a sequence of no more than 7 minutes from one film as the focus for the study. The film should be one that is well known to you and that you feel comfortable discussing; it should be relatively recent and have had mainstream cinema release. (You will find the analysis difficult if you choose an obscure film or one with which you are not comfortable.) As for the sequence, choose one that makes a clear use of the micro element or elements you have selected.

The micro elements

The micro elements of a film work together to create the film's look, narrative, characters, settings and meanings. The director's choice of camerawork, editing, sound and *mise-en-scène* for a film creates what you eventually see on the screen. Micro elements are important not only for how a film appears to its audience but also for conveying different meanings. Micro elements might be used in a way the audience expects, providing a predictable experience for the viewer, or they might be used in an unusual way to make viewers think and to challenge their expectations of a film. Imagine the piece of music which you think would be attached to the villain of a film. Your expectations would probably be of an ominous, dark, maybe brooding piece. If your expectations were met, it would be clear how you were supposed to respond to that character. If the piece of music attached to the villain were lighter or sadder, rather than chilling, you might have to revise your expectations. Make sure that, in your essays, you not only identify and describe the micro elements you have chosen but also discuss how they are used and the effects of this use on the audience.

Below are definitions for each of the micro elements. As you read through these and the examples given, note down your own examples of films that use micro elements in similar ways. If you have already chosen the film and the 7 minutes you wish to study, you could make notes on how each of the micro elements is used in your sequence.

Sound

Sound is an essential element within any film and is integral to the creation of meaning. The first distinction to be understood is the difference between sound that exists within the story of a film (sound that characters may be able to hear) and sound that has been added to the film at the post-production stage (sound which the characters cannot hear). The first type of sound is called **diegetic**. Voices, traffic noises, car radios and doors creaking are all examples of diegetic sounds. The word diegesis means story, so diegetic sound is that which exists within the story of a film. Music on soundtracks and voice-overs are examples of the type of sound added to a film in post-production. These are called **non-diegetic** sound, because they do not exist within the story of a film. Diegetic and non-diegetic sound have a range of functions which are explored more fully below. Two introductory examples are:

- **Diegetic sound** — the chaos of rain sounds, traffic noises and blaring radios of the introduction to the nameless city in David Fincher's film *Se7en*, create a feeling of unease, discomfort and insecurity for the viewer.
- **Non-diegetic sound** — the shrill, repeated violin sounds which Bernard Hermann created as the soundtrack for the shower scene in Hitchcock's *Psycho* are a musical echo of the knife stabs.

Many terms that you need to know in association with film sound are highlighted in this section. In order to explore how both diegetic and non-diegetic sound exist in films in an easily comprehensible way, it is useful to consider how they function to produce meaning within four key areas: character, narrative, genre and setting.

Sound and character

Both diegetic and non-diegetic sound can be used to give the viewer information about character. Non-diegetic music on a soundtrack, for example, can be attached to a particular character in a film to give information about personal qualities or a state of mind. Music specific to a particular character is called a **character theme**. The famous piece of music for the shark in *Jaws*, for example, introduces the actual or potential presence of the shark; we do not need to see the creature in order to know that it is present. The music has a relentless, unstoppable and menacing quality which generates tension and fear in the audience.

Diegetic sounds, too, can become synonymous with particular characters and signal their presence in a film. In *Scream**, for example, the killers harass their victims on the telephone. The opening image of the film is of a phone ringing and the character who answers it becomes the first victim. From then on in the film, the sound of a phone ringing becomes associated with the disjointed voice of the killer contacting the next victim. This everyday and banal sound thus becomes threatening and creates tension for the audience.

Sound and narrative

The way in which sound can have an effect on narrative is often quite subtle. A **sound bridge**, for example, where a non-diegetic or diegetic sound is carried from one scene

through into the next one, can be an effective way for the filmmaker to suggest a link between the two scenes. A non-diegetic character theme used when a certain character is present in a scene, may continue into a scene where that character is no longer present. This could imply that, even though the character is absent, he/she is present in the mind of the character in the next scene.

Sound can help us predict what the content of a story will be. Lasse Hallstrom's *Chocolat*, for example, opens with the kind of non-diegetic soundtrack you might expect to introduce a fairy tale; we expect almost magical happenings. In fact, the chocolate of the film's title does, indeed, bring about almost magical changes in the inhabitants of the village.

Voice-overs are an example of non-diegetic sound which can affect the way we understand narrative elements. They act as a guide to our narrative understanding, provide a commentary on the events depicted and give us information which might not be available purely through the film's visual element. The voice of Lester Burnham in Sam Mendes's *American Beauty** introduces us to the events in the film and to his family — but also tells us that he is already dead. We do not see his death until the very end of the film but we are warned about it from the beginning. Don't forget, however, that voice-overs can be unreliable; they allow a filmmaker to control the amount of narrative information a viewer has access to. Leonard Shelby, the narrator of Christopher Nolan's film *Memento*, for example, cannot remember recent events and is, therefore, completely unreliable when giving information about what has happened.

Sound and genre

Sound is an essential part of the way in which genre is established in a film, whether horror, Western, science fiction or romantic comedy. The non-diegetic soundtrack is an important indicator of genre. Van Gelis's haunting, industrial-sounding music for *Blade Runner*, for example, has an 'other world', futuristic feel to it, which identifies the film as a piece of science fiction. Bernard Hermann's signature piece for Hitchcock's *Vertigo* constantly spirals towards climaxes which never happen; it seems to avoid giving the viewer a safe resolution. Thrillers often pivot on mystery, complex plot-lines and protagonists who are bewildered and confused until the end of the narrative. The music in *Vertigo* reflects this mystery, confusion and postponed resolution perfectly.

Diegetic sounds can aid in genre identification, too. The sounds of horses' hooves, saddle straps, guns and stagecoaches would suggest a Western to the viewer. The sounds of creaking doors, hooting owls, wind and screams would indicate a Gothic horror film.

Sound and setting

It is important for a filmmaker to create a clear sense of place. The atmosphere of an environment, the historical period and country in which the action is set can all be evoked through sound. The use of diegetic sound in *The Blair Witch Project*, for example, is an essential tool in the creation of meaning. As the protagonists move deeper into the forest, the silence becomes overwhelming, so that the cracking of a twig strikes fear into them and the voices and screams that they begin to hear are terrifying. The silences, punctuated only by disturbing sounds, create an atmosphere of isolation and terror for the protagonists and the foreboding of a chilling resolution for the viewer.

Non-diegetic sound can generate information about setting, as in Maurice Jarre's famous grand and awe-inspiring music soundtrack for *Lawrence of Arabia*, for example, which evokes the vastness and power of the desert setting. Gabriel Yared's music for the opening shots of *The English Patient* — a plane flying over the desert — evokes the expanse, grandeur and, in this film, the romance of the place.

Your sequence

Make sure that you discuss the function of music to create meaning in the four areas described above. Identify any unusual uses of sound in the films you have chosen, for instance sound that works against your expectations. The use of **contrapuntal** sound could provide an interesting topic for discussion — sound that does not seem to 'fit' with the scene or images you are watching. The song, 'Over the rainbow', for example, is used in a shoot-out scene in John Woo's *Face/Off*. It seems contradictory to the violence of the scene but it is being used to calm a frightened boy. The song begins as diegetic sound in the child's headphones but spills out onto the non-diegetic sound track as if to highlight the innocence and vulnerability of the boy in such an environment. In Danny Boyle's *Trainspotting**, the scene of Renton in his squalid room, attempting to give up 'junk', is accompanied by a soundtrack of classical music. This seeming contradiction of tone allows for an even greater degree of contrast between the affluent world often associated with classical music and the drug-saturated deprivation of Renton's life.

> ### Key words
>
> diegetic; non-diegetic; character theme; sound bridge; contrapuntal sound

Mise-en-scène

Mise-en-scène is a French term which literally means everything that is 'put into the scene'. Imagine a freeze-frame — all the elements that have been placed in front of the camera in that freeze-frame are elements of *mise-en-scène*.

Mise-en-scène includes:
- settings
- decor
- props
- lighting
- costume
- make-up
- colour
- body language and movement

The use of *mise-en-scène* elements encourages the viewer to 'read' a scene in a partic-ular way. Your chosen film sequence will use these micro elements in order to generate specific meanings. *Mise-en-scène* can offer the viewer information and meanings connected to character, genre, atmosphere, mood, place, space and time. Elements of *mise-en-scène* may be repeated within a film; they may also change. You should identify carefully the elements that are constant and those that change and consider why the changes occur.

Settings
Settings within a film can evoke many kinds of responses. They can mirror the emotions of a character, establish place and time, and offer information about themes within a film. Consider the snowbound, bleak landscape of the Coen brothers' *Fargo*, for example. From the opening shots, which are almost completely filled with snow, we have a sense of a place which is both isolated and isolating. The monotony of the snowy landscape and its monotone palette act as a counterpoint to the dramatic and violent events that unfold. The bright picket fences, well-kept lawns and neat houses of the setting for Sam Mendes's *American Beauty** are too perfect and provide a picture-book surface for the dissatisfaction of the characters.

Decor
The room in which a scene occurs can add meaning to the event shown. The decor of a room (wallpaper, furniture and layout) can mirror a character's psychological state. Norman Bates's study in Hitchcock's *Psycho* is full of old furniture and stuffed birds, the decor has no vitality, the room is almost mummified. In James Cameron's *Titanic*, the different decks present the class differences between the passengers: the upper decks are opulent and expensively furnished while the rooms of the lower-deck passengers are simple and without luxury.

Props
The objects included in a scene are essential in the generation of meaning, giving information about genre, historical period or character. One of the ways in which we can identify the genre of a film is through the props used: in *The Matrix* (Wachowski brothers, 1999) space ships, futuristic weaponry and advanced computer systems all indicate that the genre is science fiction. The puppets used by the central character in Spike Jonze's *Being John Malkovich* indicate a man dissatisfied with his own life, playing out his fantasies through the wooden characters. Think about the props in the scene you have chosen and analyse what you can deduce from them.

Lighting
Lighting is essential in conveying the mood or atmosphere of a scene. The viewer can be drawn to objects or characters that are brightly lit or can be made nervous by shadows and obscured parts of the film frame. The three main types of light used in cinematography are:
- the **key light** — usually the brightest light
- the **back light** — often used behind characters to make them seem more rounded and less one-dimensional

- the **filler light** — this helps to soften harsh shadows which might be thrown by the key light or back light

These lights can be directed from different angles to produce a range of effects.

In **underlighting**, the source of light within a scene comes from below. This often has a distorting effect on the object or character being lit and can be used to make the character or object seem threatening. Horror films often use underlighting in order to make the audience feel scared of a character or fearful of an object.

In **toplighting**, the light comes from above. It is often used to highlight the actor's features and make them appear more glamorous.

In **backlighting**, the light source comes from behind a character. If the only lighting in a scene is backlighting, silhouettes are created. This effect could give a character an air of mystery and create tension in the audience.

Some genres of film use specific types of lighting to create effects. Scenes in examples of *film noir* often use pools of light, rather than full lighting, to generate the mystery and suspense which is at the heart of all films of this genre. Identify what the dominant type of lighting is in the sequence you have chosen and then consider what meanings it helps to generate.

Key words

key light; back light; filler light; underlighting; toplighting; backlighting

Costume

The costumes are important in the creation of historical time, characters' state of mind and status, and in the generation of place. The different clothes worn in each of the stories within Stephen Daldry's *The Hours*, for example, clearly define the time periods as the 1920s, the 1940s and the 1990s. Changes in costume for a particular character during a film can indicate anything from a change in fortunes to a shift in political affiliations. Julia Roberts's costume shift in *Pretty Woman*, for example, carries particular meaning and signals her character's transition from street-hustling prostitute to tycoon's girlfriend. Within this kind of Cinderella story, the shedding of one set of clothes for another signals a change in social status and, perhaps, of attitude.

Make-up

Make-up is an essential tool for all actors but it can also be used to generate particular meanings. Tom Hanks's make-up in *Philadelphia* shows us the physical ravages of AIDS and adds to our sympathy for his plight. The make-up and prosthetics worn by Willem Dafoe as the Green Goblin in Sam Raimi's *Spiderman* are grotesque and frightening: we are left in no doubt that he is the villain within this narrative.

Subtle differences in the use of make-up can indicate historical period. The 1960s scenes in the Austin Powers films, for example, are given more realism by the heavy eye-liner and bright lipstick shades from that period.

Colour

Colours can be used to great effect within films, dominating in certain scenes or identifying people and objects. Your chosen sequence may seem bled of colour, leaving only dull or neutral tones, to indicate, possibly, a depressed situation or character. On the other hand, your scene may be brimming with colours, indicating a positive atmosphere and state of mind of the characters. Consider the startling colour change when Dorothy enters the land of Oz in *The Wizard of Oz*. Her 'real' life is depicted in black and white, but her fantasy world is technicoloured. The escapism and dream quality of Oz is clear to see. The colour red becomes significant in certain scenes of Steven Spielberg's *Schindler's List*, as the red of a young girl's coat is highlighted against the black and white of the rest. When we see a flash of red within a mound of bodies, the plight of the girl under the Nazi regime is highlighted starkly.

Body language and movement

The way a character moves, sits or stands can transmit information about feelings and attitudes. The aimless wandering through the streets of New York of Travis Bickle in Martin Scorsese's *Taxi Driver**, for example, is symptomatic of his state of mind. He feels alienated and isolated and this is translated into his purposeless walking.

Blocking is a term which you will need to be aware of in your discussions about character. If a character is partially hidden from view by a wall or a tree or another character, he/she is 'blocked'. If the viewer is unable to see what a character is doing, a response of concern or fear may result. Imagine you are watching a horror film and the actions of the killer are obscured from view; your imagination creates the worst reading of that character's actions.

Cinematography

Cinematography includes everything connected with the camera. You need to discuss the **shot type** used, the **camera position** and the **camera movement**. The other important aspect of cinematography you should discuss is framing. When a filmmaker frames a shot, he/she is making a decision about not only what should be included in a particular shot but also what percentage of the shot is taken up with each element. You need to study all these elements carefully when analysing cinematography in the sequence you have chosen.

Types of shot

Every film is made up of shots which are edited together to provide scenes. Each shot type has a function, but remember that filmmakers may 'play' with the expected function of a shot in order to draw a different response from the viewer.

- The **extreme long shot** (ELS) — in this either the human characters are minute within the setting or the shot is purely of the setting. Films often use ELSs as an introduction to the place in which the action will occur.

- The **long shot** (LS) — the characters can be seen in entirety in their environment. The LS is often used in a film to associate different characters with particular environments.
- The **medium shot** (MS) — this shows the characters from the knees up. It is an extremely common type of shot and is often used for groups of people conversing.
- The **medium close-up** (MCU) — this gives a chest-up view of individuals and is often used to shoot two characters in conversation.
- The **close-up** (CU) — this frames the entire head, hand or foot of a character or a part of an object. If there is a specific element within a scene — a clue, for example — or if the filmmaker wishes the audience to see the emotions on the face of a character, a close-up is used.
- The **extreme close-up** (ECU) — this presents only a portion of a face or object. It can be used to focus the viewer's attention on frightened or tearful eyes or to obscure the identity of a character by only showing a fragment of a face.
- The **establishing shot** — this is the opening shot of a film or a film sequence. An ELS or LS might be used to introduce the viewer to the place of the film's action.
- The **master shot** — this includes all of the action in a particular sequence. At the editing stage, any close-ups on characters or medium close-ups of conversations can be inserted into the master shot. The master shot acts as a constant background of action which is punctuated with other shots.
- The **cutaway shot** — this is of something outside the main action of a scene, which is used to join two sections of the main scene together. The cutaway shot could be of a reaction to the main action by an onlooker or it might be of another character who is not part of the main action but has a connection to it. This type of shot is designed to encourage the viewer to make connections between what is happening in one part of a film and characters or objects in another part.
- The **cut-in shot** — this cuts into a small part of the main scene. The cut-in shot might be of a significant detail in the scene, for example a clue or a weapon. This type of shot allows the filmmaker to highlight significant details within a scene.

Camera position

The position of the camera when a shot is filmed has a significant effect on the meanings that are generated. Within the sequence you have chosen, consider whether the camera is positioned at eye level, at a low angle, at a high angle or whether the audience is being positioned as if it were a character via a point-of-view shot.

- For an **eye-level shot**, the camera is positioned at chest or head height. This generates a sense of normality for the viewers, who are used to viewing events from eye level.
- A **low-angle shot** positions the camera below eye level, looking up at a character, object or the action within a scene. This type of shot tends to make what is shot look powerful or even threatening.
- A **high-angle shot** places the camera above eye level, looking down on characters or action. What the audience views therefore seems vulnerable or insignificant.

- A **point-of-view** shot (POV) presents action as if from the viewpoint of a particular character. This can encourage the audience to identify with characters or empathise with their situation.

Camera movement

The movement of the camera can add meaning to a scene and encourage the viewer to read a scene in a particular way. Movement may be actual or, in the case of a zoom shot, generated by the use of a particular lens. If a camera **pans** (the base of the camera remains static, but the 'head' rotates horizontally from right to left or left to right) across a particular scene, the filmmaker may be inviting the viewer to notice details or characters within that scene. If the camera **tilts** (the base remains stationary, but the head of the camera moves vertically up or down), the viewer may have been positioned as a character within the film, looking up and down a building or another character. A **tracking shot** occurs when the whole camera moves in, out or sideways to follow the action. The camera may be mounted on a track or a dolly (a tripod with wheels), or a Steadicam hand-held unit may be used. Tracking shots enable filmmakers to follow moving action or characters through scenes.

Key words

shot type; camera movement; camera position; framing; pan; tilt; tracking shot

Editing

Editing is the process of selecting and arranging shots to reproduce the scenes in the screenplay. A film will be organised or edited in a way that attempts to hide the fact that scenes are made up of many different shots. The type of editing in the sequence you have chosen for your micro study can be used to give information about characters, narrative and the messages conveyed.

The first element of editing which you will need to discuss is **shot transition**. One scene or shot may move to another by using a cut. This is the simplest form of transition and is shown by an instantaneous change from one shot to the next. Cuts are often not noticed by the viewer: a film can be viewed without the viewer being distracted by the mechanics of the editing. A **dissolve** is a type of transition that involves one shot fading out, while another shot fades in. At some point both shots are visible briefly on the screen. The dissolve may be used to make a connection in the mind of the viewer between one shot and another. A **fade** is the gradual darkening or lightening of an image until it becomes black or white. One shot does not move into another, but into a blank (black or white) screen. In a **wipe**, one shot seems to wipe the other off the screen. It is often used to move the film between different locations experiencing the same time. The type of transitions used in the film you have chosen may indicate connections between certain times, places and characters. You need to be aware of two main types of editing. The first is **continuity editing**, which ensures that the narrative of the film is continuous and unbroken. Continuity editing preserves the chronology of the story in a film and gives the impression of real time. Time does not jump around with continuity editing; it moves forward in the way the audience would expect. The types of film you choose for your micro study will probably be continuity edited. They may involve flashbacks, but ultimately the story moves forwards in time in a way that is easily understandable. **Montage editing** is entirely different from continuity editing. The term describes rapid movement between different images, which may seem to conflict with each other. The generation of real time is not the goal of a montage sequence. The conflicting images you see are used to generate *meaning* rather than an approximation of real time. They may seem to have no connection with each other but, viewed so closely together and at such speed, you may find that the filmmaker is making a point about or offering an opinion on a particular subject.

Key words and examples

transition; cut; dissolve; fade; wipe; continuity editing; montage editing

Writing your micro study essay

As with any writing that you do during your film studies course, it is essential that your micro essay is clear, well organised and has examples to back up the points you make. You have between 1,000 and 1,500 words in which to analyse your chosen sequence and you should make every word count. Do not tell the story of your film or describe the events in your sequence. The micro elements you choose should connect in some way, so that you can make related points. *Mise-en-scène* and editing, for example, come at opposite ends of the film-making process and so are more difficult to relate than *mise-en-scène* and cinematography, which come at the same stage. This piece of writing should exhibit analysis throughout. Below are guidelines for organising your essay effectively.

The specification instruction is as follows:

Focus on how one or more of *mise-en-scène*, cinematography, editing and sound create meaning and generate response in a film sequence of no more than 7 minutes.

Introduction

Your introduction could begin by outlining some of the ways in which micro features can generate meaning and create a response in the viewer. Depending on which micro elements you choose, you could highlight how narrative sense, time, mood, atmosphere and characters' state of mind, for example, can be generated by particular uses of micro features. The end of your introduction should state the title, director and date of the film you are studying and the sequence that you have chosen.

The main body of your essay

In these central paragraphs you should explore the micro features you have chosen in relation to the meanings generated in your sequence. Work through your sequence systematically and identify the different ways in which sound, *mise-en-scène*, cinematography or editing create the meanings you identify. There may be many variations in the use of micro features in your sequence and you need to explore how and why these variations occur. Don't forget to use the specific terminology you have learnt in order to make your points.

The easiest way to begin writing your essay is to note down the micro features you have chosen. For each of your micro elements you could then create three lists. The first list should be of *terminology* you may wish to use for the particular micro feature. The second list should be of all the potential *areas of meaning* that the use of your micro elements could indicate. Your third list should be of *textual examples* from your film which relate to the areas of meaning in your second list.

> ### Example
>
> **Micro element: sound**
> **List 1**
> diegetic; non-diegetic; sound bridge; character theme; contrapuntal sound
> **List 2**
> Possibly used to: create mood/atmosphere; describe characters' state of mind; predict the entrance of a character; indicate that one character is thinking about another; establish genre; establish place; establish time
> **List 3**
> (A list of examples from your sequence which show sound generating the elements in list 2.)

Having completed your lists, you will have possible sub-topics which you can use to begin each paragraph. You will find that your micro elements often share 'uses' and this will enable you to connect micro features within your essay. For example, both sound and *mise-en-scène* can be used to create information about a character's state of mind. Rather than discuss the same feature of sound and *mise-en-scène* at two separate points in your essay, you could create one paragraph which discusses the use of both micro elements to produce the same kind of information for the audience.

Each of your paragraphs should begin with a clear point and then give a textual example to back up that point. Your paragraphs should include a comment on how the audience responds to the use of the micro element(s).

Conclusion

Your conclusion should summarise the meanings and responses generated by your chosen micro elements. You could comment, too, on whether you think they have been generated effectively.

Practical application of learning

There are two options for the practical work, based on original ideas, which you will need to submit for your Unit 1 assessment: a storyboard or a screenplay. There are 20 marks available. If you choose the storyboard option, you will need to produce between 15 and 25 different shots for a film sequence. The screenplay should be between 500 and 800 words in length, including both dialogue and directions. Work for both of the practical tasks should be presented on A4 paper, observing basic conventions (these are identified and explained within this section). As well as the practical task, you will need to complete three written tasks. The first is a 200-word (maximum) synopsis of the plot of the entire film. The second is a 200-word (maximum) account of the cinematic ideas you plan to use in the practical task. The third is a 400–500-word reflection on your intended meanings within the practical work and the responses to the practical task which you have received from friends and fellow students.

Begin your practical task with a brainstorm of ideas. Think about the types of film you enjoy and what makes them enjoyable. You do not have to restrict yourself to attempting to create a new Hollywood product — you could create a more unusual film. Think about sequences from films that you have been impressed by and consider the cinematic ideas that made them impressive. You might decide on a genre of film that you enjoy and brainstorm a list of conventions which that genre uses. Don't try to create a sequel to an existing film or try to copy too closely a film that you admire. Be original.

The screenplay

Screenplays are used to give visual information, so the directions they include are as important as the dialogue. Try to balance the amount of dialogue to the directions; 400 words of each would provide a good balance.

Content and purpose

A screenplay includes everything that is necessary for a film to be made: information about characters, dialogue, action, locations, props, lighting and camera shots and angles. Once you have decided which sequence from your film you are going to trans-late into a screenplay, decide on the main characteristics of the sequence. Is it character-centred or action-centred? Is it an introductory sequence, a sequence of climax or one of resolution of the plot? Is the purpose to show an important conflict between characters or to present the journey of characters from one setting to another? It is important that you consider these questions before you begin the practical task, as the answers will help with the directions and dialogue you include.

Planning

Begin by planning and noting down specific details of character, setting, camerawork and editing. For a genre film, be aware of the generic elements that might be visible in your sequence. An opening sequence for a romantic comedy, for example, would include an introduction to the (at this stage) separate lives of the main characters as well as indications of any hurdles which they will have to overcome in order to be together, for example existing partners who are unsuitable or social differences which mean that the characters exist in different kinds of worlds.

Characters

The characters must seem real. What are their names? What do they look like? How do they move? What are they wearing? What is their body language within the action? Do they have any particular features of body language which make them unusual? You will need to give enough information to make them seem alive on the page. If the character is the chief protagonist, how can the audience differentiate him or her from the rest of the characters?

Locations

Think about the locations. You will need to place your characters in a setting that is believable and have them act in that setting in a credible way. A character's vulner-ability would show up in a setting that is new or uncomfortable for them. You might give this information to your audience through hunched body language or halting, nervous speech.

Settings

Settings relate information concerning the genre, the atmosphere of the scene and the environment of characters, so give accurate descriptions of place and setting. If the sequence takes place in a London pub, for example, you would need to describe the light, the sounds, the smells, the number of customers, the objects on some of the tables. You could research details for your screenplay by visiting whatever setting you describe and noting the elements which make that setting recognisable. If the weather is significant, consider the effect of the weather on the setting. Can rain be seen dripping down windows? Does the wind fill the street scenes with blowing leaves? Does a snowstorm make the action within your sequence difficult for the viewer to see? This kind of detail will help to create a believable and interesting environment for your audience. You could consider whether or not the setting is symbolic, in some way, of the character's state of mind or the mood of the sequence. An unhappy character could be shown battling through crowds in a street, insignificant within the scene. A confused character may become lost in their environment and incapable of finding their way. Use your settings to give as much information as possible — they can deliver meaning as successfully as dialogue.

Dialogue

Dialogue and directions work together in order to create meaning. A long speech, with no directions, will seem flat and bland. Think about the content, rhythms and tone of ordinary conversations. People do not always wait for others to finish before they begin speaking and there is no reason why your characters should be allowed to complete their sentences before being interrupted. If you have established your character as being from a specific place and as having a particular state of mind, these features will need to be reflected in their words. It is not a good idea to attempt to recreate regional accents and dialects unless you are expert in them, as they are very difficult to write down. Age affects how characters speak, as do thoughts and motivations in the sequence. Who a character is speaking to is a significant factor. You might need to change the patterns of speech for a character who begins the sequence talking to a friend and ends it with a discussion with a parent.

Voice-overs and interior monologues

You could include a section of thought in your sequence, where a character withdraws from the action and comments on events in voice-over. What a character might say in the privacy of his or her own head might be completely different in language, tone and content from what someone would say out loud. For a voice-over, decide upon not only what is said and how it is said, but also the reliability of the voice-over narrator — is this version of events different from what the visual elements of the film suggest?

Technical directions

In addition to details of character, setting and dialogue, your screenplay should include notes about camera angles and sound. Your study of the micro elements of film has equipped you with a knowledge of the potential use, function and meaning of camerawork, editing and sound. Your descriptions of setting will already have utilised your knowledge of *mise-en-scène*.

You should bring your knowledge of other micro elements into the practical task, too. Think about the movement of your sequence. Are there any sections where the pace needs to pick up or slow down? You could use quick cuts to indicate pace or dissolves to create a sense of slow, fluid movement. Your sequence might require reaction shots from different characters and you might use a cut to close-up in order to show the emotion on a character's face. An introductory sequence would require an extreme long shot or a long shot to introduce a setting.

Layout

You need to observe certain conventions in the structure and layout of your screenplay. Most screenplays are written in the third person (he, she etc.) and in the present tense (walks, rather than walked). Each scene is preceded by information about

whether the scene is interior (inside) or exterior (outside), the location and the time of day — for example:

EXT. BRIDGET'S GARDEN. EARLY EVENING

The next type of information to include is detail of the setting, camera angles, sound and any character present in the scene and what they are doing. If we have not already been introduced to a character, details of appearance and age should be included. If the sequence is from a point in the film at which the audience already knows what the character looks like, detail of physical appearance can be more limited — for example:

Medium shot of BRIDGET as she lies on the scorched grass in
her back garden, reading a book. She is not concentrating
fully on her novel, as she is transfixed by a bee which has
landed on one of the flowers in the flowerbed in front of her.
The air is full of late summer sounds: insects, a nearby ice
cream van and the sounds of children's laughter from a park
close by. Her sandals and dress are lying in a heap next to
where she is sunbathing in her green swimming costume.

If a character begins speaking, their name, information about how they are speaking and what they say are usually centred on the page. The information about how a character speaks is often given in italics — for example:

MOLLY, BRIDGET'S MOTHER
(*in a tone of annoyance*)

Your aunt has arrived. The least you can do is
come in and say hello.

Your screenplay will include passages that give directions as well as those that state and describe dialogue. Make sure that you include every possible detail to help your reader visualise the scene.

Key words

directions; dialogue

The storyboard

The first thing to note, if you are producing a storyboard, is that you do not have to be a brilliant artist to create something effective, so try to draw your storyboard yourself. It is the cinematic ideas that are marked, not the drawing. (You are allowed to get someone else to draw it for you if there is no other option, but in this case you would need to submit your own preliminary version of the storyboard as well as the 'commissioned' one.)

Content

The marks you receive for your storyboard are for the way it communicates meaning to the viewer. This is done primarily through the drawings, but you need to include other information: camera movement and angle within the shot, editing information, figure movement within the shot and three types of sound (speech, non-diegetic noise/music, diegetic noise/music).

Function

The function of a storyboard is to give information to the director about the camera shots and movements relevant to each scene. The storyboard should present a fluid indication of how one shot moves to the next within the scene. Information about characters' movements in individual shots, the sound involved and the edit type are essential to the realisation of the sequence. Your storyboard must make clear narrative sense.

Planning

Once you have selected the sequence, brainstorm all the information that will be relevant to your storyboard. If your film is a genre piece and your sequence requires specific generic elements, consider how to include them and how they will be shot. Bear in mind where the sequence comes in your film. Think about the distance the camera needs to be from the subject within your shot. An introductory sequence will need an establishing shot, for example, and you will probably need to use an extreme long shot or a long shot. You will need to consider the position of the characters and their roles in the sequence. Is there a powerful character others are afraid of? If so, consider a camera position (such as a low angle) which will indicate this to the viewer. If you were trying to position the viewer as if they were one of the characters in the scene, you would need to create a point-of-view shot in your storyboard.

Storyboard checklist

In order to make sure that the storyboard fulfils all the exam board's criteria and makes narrative sense, draw up a checklist of information. Below is a list of all of the types of information you need to decide upon before you begin.

Genre elements

If your film is of a particular genre, think about the character types, objects, sound elements and camera angles you associate with that genre and try to create your own version of them in your storyboard. You may have created an independent style of film, which does not fit easily into a genre category, but you should list the elements that will achieve the result you are aiming for.

Place in the narrative

It is important that you indicate the position of the sequence in your film's narrative structure. This information is relayed through your choices of dialogue, sound, camera work and editing. A fast action sequence will need a series of cuts. Intimate dialogue

will need medium close-ups. The place of the sequence within the film will dictate the choices you make.

Camera angle

Consider whether the shot you are creating needs an eye-level angle, a high angle or a low angle. Eye-level angles are often used to place the viewer in a scene, a high angle may indicate that the subject of the shot is small or vulnerable and a low-angle shot might be used to show the size or status of the character, building or object which is the subject of the shot. You should write special information about camera angles below the frame.

Camera level

Most of the time, shots are framed level. The camera is positioned so that buildings appear vertical and the horizon is horizontal. If you have chosen a sequence in which either your character or your viewer is disorientated, you might decide to create a shot that is not level. 'Canted angles' make the frame appear 'wonky' and can indicate a disturbed character viewpoint or an unreality. If you have chosen a particularly unusual camera level, include this information below the storyboard frame.

Camera height

You may have planned a shot of the feet of a character as they walk through a scene. Rather than shoot the feet from a high angle, you could create a shot where the camera is at floor level. Reinforce the information about camera height by writing the height below the frame, next to the camera angle information.

Camera distance

Camera distance is important in the creation of meaning. Close-ups have a different function from medium shots, for example. Consider the action occurring in each frame. What kind of distance does the camera need to be from the subject in order to create the right information? An extreme close-up of an eye, for example, in a thriller or horror film can relay information about the fear that a character is experiencing. Below your frame, indicate the camera distance by writing the relevant abbreviation, such as CU (close-up) or ELS (extreme long shot).

Camera movement

You need to indicate how the camera moves. Is tracking, panning or tilting of the camera necessary? For an action sequence, where you need to show the pace of a car or a train, for example, you might decide that the camera needs to follow the movement in a tracking shot. This can be done in your storyboard by putting a right- or left-facing arrow at the bottom of your frame. A point-of-view shot up or down a person or a building would need a tilt, in order to show the movement of the gaze. To indicate a tilt, place a vertical arrow within the frame, pointing up or down. A panning shot from left to right or from right to left can be used to introduce the audience to a particular setting. The arrow for a pan is horizontal, pointing in the direction of the camera movement. Explain the arrow with a note about the camera movement below the frame.

Character movement

As with camera movement, you can indicate the movement of characters with arrows in the frame. If a character is shown walking towards a building, for example, draw an arrow next to the character, pointing from the character to the building.

Sound elements

The sound elements you have chosen for each shot should be described below the frame. A diegetic noise, such as a car alarm, might be significant to the action. A non-diegetic piece of music might be essential for creating mood. This information needs to be written clearly below the shot. Any diegetic dialogue should be indicated but kept brief. One line is sufficient.

Edit type

The information you need to relay about editing can be presented clearly and simply. If your sequence has a dreamlike quality and you have decided that this is illustrated best through a series of dissolves, then you need only to write 'dissolve' between the relevant frames. A scene at the conclusion of your film might end with a fade to black. In this instance, you only need to write 'fade to black'.

Once you have decided upon all of this information, you can begin creating your storyboard. Look at the storyboards shown in the Coursework Samples section of this guide — you could use the structure and layout of the A-grade example as a template for your own work.

> **Key words and examples**
>
> frame; camera angle; camera distance; camera movement; camera height; camera level; edit type

Written work

Synopsis

Once you have decided upon the idea for your film, the first task you need to complete is the synopsis. This should be written before you begin any practical work. It must be written in the present tense, set the genre, give an outline of the plot and include the major characters and significant events, without going into details of sub-plots and secondary characters. The reader should gain enough information from the synopsis to want to see the film.

Cinematic ideas

Your account of the cinematic ideas to be developed in the sequence covered by your storyboard or screenplay extract should be written before you begin your practical work. This piece of writing includes details of the technical devices (such as camerawork, *mise-en-scène*, editing and sound) to be used within your screenplay or story-

board and the effect they are intended to have on the viewer. Within this section, you could refer to existing films and the cinematic ideas within them which have influenced your decisions for your own film. If you are planning a Western, you might discuss the use of sound elements in Sergio Leone's films, for example, as an influencing factor. The synopsis and ideas together carry 10 marks.

Evaluation

Your evaluation should be completed after you have finished your practical work. It should reflect both the intention behind your work and the responses it received. You need to discuss the meanings that you hoped to generate in your storyboard or screenplay and how effectively you think they were realised in the finished product.

You will get feedback from other members of your class, who will provide you with an informed audience for your work. Did they understand what kind of sequence you created? Did the movement of the narrative make sense to them? How did they respond to the technical choices you made? The evaluation carries 10 marks.

There are examples of the practical task written elements in the next section of this guide. Read through them before you begin writing your own; they will help you to understand what is expected.

Coursework
Samples

This section of the guide provides you with examples of the written analysis and practical work tasks which you will need to complete for the WJEC Film Studies **Unit FS1: Film — Making Meaning 1**. For each of the tasks, two answers are provided; one of A-grade standard and one of C-grade standard. It is important that you use these answers as a structure and content guide, rather than as model answers. You may choose to complete the tasks quite differently, using other examples, and achieve equally good marks. Consider the language used in the answers and the way in which the material is organised and the arguments are structured. These elements will be of most use to you when you tackle your tasks.

Each of the candidate answers is accompanied with a commentary, which indicates what is creditable in the answers and explains why the candidates received the grades they did. Pay particular attention to the skills highlighted in the commentaries and the problems identified. These comments should assist you in your coursework preparation.

Macro analysis

A-grade candidate's analysis of a sequence from *Bridget Jones's Diary*

Bridget Jones's Diary (Sharon Maguire, 2001) was originally a novel by Helen Fielding and became an extremely successful film when it was released as a romantic comedy. The film made around £41 million in the UK alone.

The storyline is funny, romantic and also safe, in that the audience knows that there will be a happy ending. From pre-release advertising and publicity, audiences could anticipate that the film would fit their expectations of the romantic comedy genre. Knowledge of the genre helps people know what to expect from a film and ensures that they will enjoy a film which they connect with examples of the genre enjoyed in the past.

In all films the story — the narrative — is important and so the way the story is told must be effective in its manipulation and presentation of characters and events. The audience needs to be able to understand the story. The narrative offers meanings connected to character actions and motivations. I have chosen to analyse the last 15 minutes of the film, where the two main characters come together and resolve their differences.

Bridget Jones's Diary was released with a target audience of women in mind. A woman is the protagonist and female audiences can relate to her experiences. Certain actors have strong links with the romantic comedy genre: Hugh Grant has a lead role and audiences would associate him with romantic comedy from his parts in *Four Weddings and a Funeral* and *Notting Hill*. (This is an important factor for the producer, especially in light of the success of these previous romantic comedies.) Hugh Grant's role in this film is slightly different in that he plays the 'cad'. However, the genre association is still beneficial for the film's producers, as they can tap into his existing romantic comedy fan base. Renée Zellweger was relatively unknown in a romantic comedy context (apart from *Jerry Maguire*), but her inclusion in the cast added an intrigue factor. Could this up-and-coming American actress play the now iconic English Bridget? Since *Bridget Jones's Diary* had been a successful newspaper column, which became a best-selling novel, even more security was added to the film's potential success at the box office.

Romantic comedy has a set of conventions to which most of the examples of this genre conform. *Bridget Jones's Diary* is the story of a single woman living in London. Both the protagonists, Bridget and Mark, lack a partner at the start of the narrative. This soon changes when Mark is with Nicola and Bridget is with Daniel, both the wrong partners and a hindrance to their union. This creates immense dramatic irony. The two protagonists are not aware of their attraction to one another, but the audience, through its knowledge of romantic comedy conventions, can see that Bridget and Mark will end the story together — but how? When they first meet, the two characters do not get on. Mark is rude and sees Bridget as beneath him. Bridget feels that Mark is dull and does not like his condescending attitude. This hostility remains until the end of the narrative. The audience knows that the couple will eventually be together, but tension and interest are sustained as the pair's hurdles are overcome. The two characters are very different; Mark is a highly paid barrister and Bridget has a relatively unprestigious job in a large publishing house. This social and economic divide constructs one of the hurdles for the couple and intrigues the audience as to how the divide will be overcome.

Bridget changes as she tries to make herself more attractive to the opposite sex. Her attempts initially 'net' Daniel, but he proves himself unworthy of her affection. The audience follows Bridget's shifts from hope to depression and back again, to an ending with Mark and hope for the future. The couple overcome their differences, learn something about themselves along the way and provide a textbook 'romcom' ending. Mark has aborted his move to America and has come back for Bridget. The series of trials which the protagonists within romantic comedies must undergo is ended successfully when he returns. Perhaps the most prominent of all romcom conventions is that the couple unite in the end, providing the viewer with met expectations of the genre and a sense of satisfaction and safety.

The audience is constantly aware of Bridget's feelings throughout the film through her diary, which is read as voice-over by Bridget. This allows Bridget's character to discuss the conventions of the romantic comedy genre in an almost self-conscious way. The audience hears how she is lonely, vulnerable, unaware of her attraction to Mark, let down by Daniel and eventually happy. This effective use of restricted narration lets us know how Bridget is feeling, which allows us to empathise with the character.

In the final sequence, conventions are used creatively to generate tension for the viewer. Bridget is at Mark's parents' ruby wedding celebration, and a remark is made about Mark and Nicola. She is overcome by her feelings and makes a fool of herself, trying to hide her outburst. She leaves and the audience is in suspense, waiting for Mark's response. The tension seems to be released when Mark comes back from America for Bridget. However, resolution is postponed by the drama of Mark reading Bridget's diary and her fears that it has offended him.

Time is compressed in the film and the viewer is presented with a whole year of Bridget's life, but the narrative highlights the events relevant to the romantic comedy storyline. This use of emotional issues and romantic confusions is typical of the romantic comedy genre. The narrative propels us towards the resolving final sequence in which misunderstandings are explained and confusions are clarified.

The narrative structure of *Bridget Jones's Diary* is almost circular. The chronology takes us from one winter to the next and allows for a condensed passage of time in which events directly relevant to Bridget can unfold. We see her engage with friends, meetings which serve to contribute to the discussions concerning relationships and allow her opportunity to explain her shifting romantic situations. Bridget exists in a state of equilibrium at the beginning of the film, but not one that is characterised by safety. Her recognisable world is shattered by the untrustworthy Daniel, who represents a disruptive element, but is reordered by the reliable and caring Mark.

A cause-and-effect model can be used to discuss how narrative works in this film. Bridget and Mark's initial conversation at the beginning of the film acts to separate the characters through a series of misunderstandings. This is necessary within the romantic comedy genre, because it provides the first of the hurdles which must be overcome. We see the consequences of each of Bridget's interactions with other characters and use our knowledge of romantic comedy conventions to predict that, although her life may be unfulfilled for a large portion of the narrative, happy resolution will come.

Bridget Jones's Diary is, therefore, typical of the romantic comedy genre. It uses the conventions an audience expects from this genre to create narrative meaning and engage the audience in the creation of the protagonists' relationship. Narrative conventions are used to reinforce our recognition of genre and edit Bridget's life experiences so that we are presented with events that we see as relevant to the genre. As a reworking of Jane Austen's novel *Pride and Prejudice*, *Bridget Jones's Diary* is a modern-day comedy of manners. Elizabeth and Darcy have become Bridget and Mark, but modern audiences have the same desire: that the couple come together in the end.

(1,269 words)

📝 This candidate shows clear understanding of the conventions of both narrative and the chosen genre and has explored them in detail. The function of narrative and genre for both the viewer and the film industry is explored with confidence and accuracy. The essay is organised clearly and presents effectively the generic elements and narrative issues of the chosen sequence which generate meaning and viewer response. The importance of the audience's knowledge of pre-existing texts for the producer of the film is explored too.

The candidate writes fluently and gives clear textual evidence for the points made. The answer contains a high degree of analytical comment and informed personal reflection — it is a clear, articulate and perceptive piece of writing, which has an original voice.

■ ■ ■

C-grade candidate's analysis of a sequence from *Shallow Hal*

When a film is made, it usually has a genre. Genre is the style or category of a film. Comedies, action films, science fiction films and musicals are all examples. Each of these genres has its own set of elements or conventions. Genres can also be broken down into subgenres. For example, slasher films are a subgenre of horror films. There are also mixed genre films, such as sci-fi/action. Narrative is also another big part of a film. It is the order or structure in which the film is presented. A typical narrative movement would be from a state of calm or equilibrium, to a state of disturbance or disruption, to a new state of peace or new equilibrium. The film I am going to analyse is *Shallow Hal* (Farrelly Brothers, 2001), which is an example of a romantic comedy.

Shallow Hal was given a PG certificate. It stars Jack Black as Hal and Gwyneth Paltrow as Rosemary. The sequence I have chosen to study is when the disruption takes place which continues throughout the majority of the rest of the film. The sequence opens with a series of clouds which have been speeded up to signify that time has passed. Events we do not need to see are left out with this compression of time. We see Hal in the context of a normal day at work. Tony Robbins is also present and is described as a TV guru. This is when the first disruption takes place. The lift suddenly stops and breaks down, with only Hal and Tony inside. Hal soon begins to panic and time is again fast-forwarded. This is indicated by the fast-moving clock. Hal describes his taste in women and after Tony has realised how shallow Hal is, he offers him hypnotism. Hal accepts. This a pivotal moment in the film, as the audience realises that Hal will not be the same again and the film's events will change after this point. To add tension, the background music of the elevator is mystical and goes with Tony's character and actions. The lift seems almost like a magical lamp, in which a genie (Tony) lives. Tony casts a spell over Hal and says: 'From this moment on, whenever you meet someone in the future, you're only going to see their inner beauty.'

From then on, Hal sees inner beauty in every woman he meets. This is presented in the film through a 'Hal's eye view' of the women. A difference between the central characters and their seeming incompatibility is essential within a romantic comedy. Hal is shallow and Rosemary is not the type of woman he would normally be interested in. The hurdle in this film, which the protagonists have to overcome, is Hal's shallow attitude. This scene is important, because it indicates an overcoming of the hurdle and makes the eventual romance between the characters of Hal and Rosemary possible. This sequence introduces the viewer to Rosemary who, through Hal's new eyes, is blonde, beautiful, slim and funny. In reality, Rosemary weighs 300 pounds, but is transformed by Hal's new, clearer vision.

Romantic comedies often exaggerate real-life situations for comic effect. In this film, Hal takes Rosemary out for lunch and her chair collapses. The chair is made of steel to exaggerate the comic effect. Hal is an extreme character who also offers comic exaggeration for the audience. He is often ridiculous and makes pathetic jokes. *Shallow Hal* fits into a new type of romantic comedy, which is more extreme and crass than films that have gone before. *There's Something About Mary* is another example of a 'romcom' which places its main characters in ridiculous scenarios.

The *mise-en-scène* of the film is colourful and happy. Although the prejudices which Hal has are quite extreme, the comedy element of the film is helped by the bright settings. The viewers know that they are watching a comedy and that eventually the problems of the narrative will be resolved.

Overall, the film *Shallow Hal* and the sequence I have chosen fit clearly into the romantic comedy genre. The audience's expectations of hurdles which will be overcome and which will lead to romantic resolution are met. The comedy elements are clear. In terms of narrative, the film offers the conventions of time compression and the movement from equilibrium to disruption to new equilibrium. This sequence asks the viewers to agree with the film's negative attitude to Hal's shallowness and to learn a lesson for themselves in how you shouldn't judge people by their appearances.

(760 words)

This answer shows good general understanding of some of the functions of genre and narrative. The candidate includes relevant personal reflection on the place of this new brand of romantic comedies and gives a useful example of a related film text (*There's Something About Mary*). The importance of genre for audience recognition and understanding is explored in some detail, although the importance of genre as a marketing tool for the film industry is not commented on. Narrative conventions are explored in some detail, with good textual examples. However, the candidate could have added a comment on 'cause and effect' to the analysis. The essay is short (under 800 words) and additional comments concerning the omitted features of narrative and genre above would have made for a more detailed study.

Micro analysis

A-grade candidate's micro analysis of a sequence from *Taxi Driver**

In order for films to be successful in attracting audiences, they need to have the right features to generate meaning and response. Cinematography is a micro feature which can generate different meanings. Different camera angles and distances from characters and objects can change the mood of a scene. For example, an extreme close-up of a killer's eyes in a horror film can generate a sense of threat and fear. Another micro feature is *mise-en-scène*, which includes everything seen in the frame, from the placement of objects to the colours chosen for the decor of a room. It is very effective for generating different atmospheres in a scene. I have chosen cinematography and *mise-en-scène* as the micro features I will analyse. The film I am studying is *Taxi Driver** (Martin Scorsese, 1976). The sequence I have chosen is when Travis meets the 13-year-old Iris for the first time, in her apartment.

This sequence occurs just after Travis has bought his collection of weapons and has talked to Iris's pimp, Sport. It begins with an impressive tilt shot of Iris's apartment block, which is supposed to surprise and intrigue the viewer. Travis and Iris disappear at the bottom of the shot. Travis is the outsider, and the screen is overwhelmed by the magnitude of the apartment block to show his insignificance and that he is but one of hundreds of others just like him. The film then cuts to a tracking shot of a murky, dark corridor, with Travis and Iris walking along it. The walls are dark and covered with graffiti, and the only light source is a single light bulb hanging solemnly at the end of the passage. This imagery changes the atmosphere and mood of the scene. The surroundings are dark and unfamiliar to Travis and he is obviously not comfortable with them. There is another cut and we see a medium shot of Travis talking to an unknown man to whom he gives money for his time with Iris. Travis and Iris then walk off screen to the right, but the camera does not cut immediately to the next scene. It stays for another few seconds on an almost empty shot. It is used again later and I will explain its significance at that time.

The next cut is to a POV shot of Travis walking into Iris's apartment. Iris stops, turns round and tells the very reluctant Travis to come in. The camera cuts again and Travis opens the door slowly and enters through the beads. Apart from being able to see Travis's anxiety at walking into a prostitute's apartment, the difference between the corridor and Iris's apartment seems shocking to him (and to the viewer). Iris is wearing summer clothes and her apartment is painted in warm pinks, reds and oranges. There are candles scattered all over the room and this not only gives it a very comfortable feeling, but indicates her attempt to eroticise her environment. Her bed is made tidily with comfortable pillows on it. All of these aspects of the room provide a contrast with Travis's own life. We have seen that his room is untidy, the walls are bare and the paint is peeling off, yet he is a fully grown adult and she is a 13-year-old prostitute. It may be gender difference or more than that. She has obviously had to look after herself from a very early age. The camera, with a close-up on his face, tracks Travis as he moves across the apartment. Subconsciously, both characters act in accordance with their stereo-types. Travis is the adult character, so he is standing. Iris is only 13, so she is sitting. This conveys to the audience that there is a difference in the maturity of the two characters.

Travis is genuinely concerned about Iris's lifestyle at such a young age. This might be the reason why both of them are positioned as they are in the shots; like a parent talking to a child. The shot-reverse shot sequence which follows shows that they are having a conversation. Iris still thinks that Travis has come to her apartment to have sex, so she stands up to initiate things. This is the first time that you really see the size difference between the two characters. They are both framed in medium close-up, but the viewer can see only Iris's head, whereas most of Travis's torso is visible. Travis is obviously not there for sex, so both sit down. The film then cuts to Iris facing the camera, with only the back of Travis's head visible. This happens frequently and might be indicative of the character of Travis. We are often not sure what he is thinking or feeling. He is quite a shadowy character, about whom we do not know as much as we think. However, this is not one of his unpredictable scenes and he does want to help Iris. Iris asks him again if he wants to have sex and, this time, with Travis and Iris both in shot, the camera pans back very quickly. This is very emotive filming, because it conveys Travis's unpredictability and how his mood has changed. It is almost as if the camera is moving away to a safe distance. Iris starts to try to undo Travis's belt. He pushes her away and begins to walk around the room. He is beginning to get paranoid and angry and this is conveyed by the fixed position of the camera on his face. Travis sits down and Iris follows suit. The camera cuts to a long shot of Travis and Iris facing each other. It is perfectly symmetrical and almost like two halves of the same person. This is in comparison with the scene before, with Travis and Betsy, where there is a distinct barrier between them, both physically and mentally.

Iris is quite difficult to understand in this scene, because she changes from being very mature and adult-like, to drifting into repetitions of how stoned she is and how she has nowhere to go. Travis stands up and so does Iris and the camera cuts to a medium close-up of both of them talking. Travis and Iris arrange to meet. He goes to leave and walks off camera, but instead of the camera cutting to the next shot, it stays on Iris and Travis walks back into shot. This is where I would like to elaborate on the point I made earlier in this essay. Travis is a very lonely man, who cannot seem to escape his loneliness wherever he goes. However, the camera is constantly on him, tracking him wherever he goes. There is only one scene in the film which he is not in. It is almost as if the loneliness he is trying to escape from is conveyed as a metaphor by the camera he cannot escape. At one point he manages to escape the camera for a split second, but it catches up with him again very quickly.

As Travis leaves Iris's apartment, there is a point of view shot of him walking towards the man (previously seen in the corridor) coming out of the darkness. Travis hands over the ten-dollar bill, which Sport gave him in the taxi earlier. This is significant, because it shows that not only is Travis uncomfortable with prostitution, but that he might provide a threat to Sport. The camera tilts down, watching Travis's hand movement, as if suggesting that he might be about to do something unpredictable. The camera cuts to a medium shot of Travis walking down the stairs and exiting the building and then cuts to another medium shot of the mysterious man entering the darkness of the corridor once more. The sequence ends with a suspicious air.

This sequence shows the viewer that Travis can care for another human being. The cinematography in this scene is on the whole quite placid, but does relay added information to the audience about Travis's caring side. The *mise-en-scène* sets the scene for Iris's character. It is a pivotal scene in the film and the micro features really help to present the blossoming relationship between Iris and Travis.

(1,373 words)

✐ This candidate has chosen a difficult sequence to analyse, but pays excellent attention to significant details of cinematography and *mise-en-scène*. The essay offers a high level of thoughtful, reflective analysis throughout. The writing is clear and terminology is used accurately. Close analysis is sustained and the candidate does not resort to description. Points made concerning cinematography and *mise-en-scène* are discussed fully, including speculation about viewer reception. The candidate explores the generation of meaning through micro features with confidence. Simple deductions concerning meaning are avoided by thoughtful discussion of the changing nature of the meanings produced.

■ ■ ■

C-grade candidate's micro analysis of a sequence from *American Beauty**

Micro features can give a film meaning and direction. They concern the small details of films. They cover the sound that accompanies a film, the way the camera moves to show a scene, what is in the frame and the way the film is edited together at the end. *Mise-en-scène* means what is 'put into the scene'. It covers everything in a single frame from lighting, to make-up and colour. These choices allow the director to encourage a certain interpretation of a scene. Cinematography is the way the camera moves in a scene. The viewer only sees what the camera shows. This allows the director to change the audience's view on such things as people. The film I am studying is *American Beauty**. It was directed by Sam Mendes and released in 1999. I am concentrating on the opening sequence.

At the very beginning of the film, we see a scene that is repeated later in the film. We don't know this yet and think that it sets up the whole story. It is of digital video footage of Jane saying how much she hates her dad. When asked by a mystery person (later revealed to be Ricky) if she wants him to kill him, she says 'Yeah'. As a viewer, I thought this set up the film as Ricky's journey to kill Lester. It is not until later that we realise that what we have seen so far was leading up to Jane's conversation with Ricky at the start of the film. In terms of cinematography, the way the camera moves and the quality of the image show it as DV footage, while the *mise-en-scène* is quite sparse so it concentrates on Jane in the frame. All of this makes the viewer concentrate on what Jane is saying.

In the DV footage, the light is coming from the left. It illuminates only one side of Jane's face. This gives the scene a dark, morbid feel, which is appropriate as they are talking about killing Lester. After this scene, the words 'American Beauty' appear on the screen.

We then cut to a high-angle establishing shot of Lester's neighbourhood. It slowly moves down over the neighbourhood, like a plane entering Lester's world. This could be Lester's ghost. We think we know that Ricky is going to kill Lester and when we first see Lester, he tells us that in less than a year he'll be dead. This scene confirms what we believe we know about the film: that it's about Ricky killing Lester. The film cuts to a crane shot of Lester in bed. We hear Lester's voice-over, saying that in less than a year he'll be dead. This is referring to the opening DV footage. It also re-establishes that the film is about Ricky killing Lester. In bed, Lester is all by himself. His wife Carolyn has got up and left him. No one bothered to wake him. This shows his family does not care about him. It makes the audience feel sorry for Lester and how bad his life is. Using a crane shot shows that Lester is low down on his family ladder. Everyone is above him. This is a cinematography point and is used to show what Lester feels about his life.

We then get a crab shot of Lester putting his slippers on — a low-angle shot under the bed, showing confined spaces. This is how Lester feels about his life, that he is always being confined and kept in place by the people around him. When we see Lester in the shower the camera slowly pans around. Lester in the shower cubicle is in another prison. This film is all about prisons. The prisons used are metaphorical. Characters in this film often feel that they are being controlled.

The film then shows an ECU of a red rose from Carolyn's garden. Red is a predominant colour within the film. In Carolyn's garden, we see the red of the rose and the door, the blue of the window shutters and the white of the slates of the house — the colours of the American flag. The garden shows that Carolyn aspires to the American dream. All of this shows that from the outside a family can appear loving and caring, but if you look closer the appearance seems to fall apart. This is a *mise-en-scène* point because it shows that what is in the frame indicates Carolyn's desire for the American dream. 'Look closer' is the film's tag line. It invites the audience to forget any preconceptions they have and to see what is really happening.

Having seen Lester's view of his life and his prisons, we move to Carolyn. Carolyn wants to be seen as perfect. She doesn't want people to know what her family is really like. When she is speaking to Jim, she puts on a very happy tone of voice. Jim is also trying to be nice, by asking about her roses. While they talk, the camera focuses in on Lester at the window. He is behind the bars of the window — another example of being in a prison.

When we first see Jane, she is looking at breast enlargements on the internet. She is shown to be a typical teenager — self-conscious about her looks and full of hate for her parents. She leaves her room and we cut to a CU of Carolyn beeping her horn. Carolyn tells Jane that she looks unattractive and when we see Lester, he drops his suitcase. Compared with the neat and presentable appearance of Jim, Lester looks scruffy and a mess. Carolyn is unimpressed by Lester, because he has made her late for work. In the car, Lester is in the back seat. Carolyn is driving. She is the head of the family and in control. In the back, Lester looks squashed. He is in another confined space. The camera shows the scenery passing by really fast. This is like Lester's life. It is going past so fast and he has done nothing with it. This is also a *mise-en-scène* point, because we can see how Lester feels and how others feel about him. It gets the viewer to sympathise with him. After the car sequence, we cut to Lester at work.

Everything in the opening sequence sets up the rest of the film. It shows how Lester and the rest of his family are trapped in their own prisons. The film is about them breaking out of their prisons and becoming somebody. You can see that Lester feels trapped in his own world by the use of confined spaces and bars. The shot of his slippers is from under the bed. We see him in a shower cubicle and in the car he is squashed up in the back. When he looks out to see Carolyn talking to Jim, the bars on the windows put his face in a box.

By using micro features, Sam Mendes is able to get the viewers to feel sorry for Lester. They can relate some of the elements in the movie to their own lives. The micro features enable Mendes to hint at what is beneath the perfect surface of the American dream.

(1,217 words)

📝 This candidate offers some concise and accurate comments about the use of chosen micro elements and the potential meanings generated. The scene is analysed in a systematic way, with good consideration of potential audience response. Appreciation of different aspects of *mise-en-scène* is evident and terminology is used with accuracy. However, the answer does not have the sustained close analysis needed for higher grades. Although there are passages of excellent analysis, there are repetitions of certain points, while not all comments are explained fully or explored. Other aspects of *mise-en-scène*, such as lighting and blocking, could have been identified. At times, cinematography elements are identified, but not analysed fully.

Screenplay

A-grade candidate's screenplay analysis of *The Ninja*

Synopsis

The year is 2025; a ninja has brutally murdered five high-class businessmen using a samurai sword. The police have several clues as to who the ninja is. Before the police have time to process all of the clues, the ninja strikes again. After yet another murder, the police eventually track the ninja down. They discover that the ninja is in fact an officer in the police force and that she was created genetically by the government to become a new fighting force against terrorism. She was trained as a superhuman ninja, but when the experiments failed they wiped her memory and gave her a job in the police force.

When some big businessmen were employing hackers to look at secret government files, they found out about the ninja. They found her and brainwashed her to carry out murders for them, using her ninja skills. In the mornings after her crimes, she could not remember what she had done.

The police discover the truth about the businessmen. The ninja is deprogrammed and can now control her skills. The police force, with the help of the ninja, raid the corporate skyscraper. The men are on the top floor, there is a fight and the ninja kills the men. She then becomes a new fighting force for the police.

(216 words)

Cinematic ideas

My screenplay scene comes just before the climax of the film. It is action-packed, with little dialogue. The first shot is supposed to be dramatic and intense. The police helicopter in the shot will help the audience identify that it is a police situation. The camera will then drop to the ground. When the camera drops, the audience hears the sound of wind rushing past, making the scene seem even more intense and exciting. This is similar to the effects generated in other action films, such as Sam Raimi's *Spiderman*.

The music throughout the scene will be orchestral and powerful. When the police team and the ninja enter the skyscraper, the room needs to be introduced quickly. This will be done by giving the audience a view from the CCTV cameras. To show this, the screen will be slightly fuzzy, with horizontal lines. It will also have a green tint to it.

When the ninja is being shot at and is darting around the room, the action will go into slow motion. The camera will circle the room. By the time all of the guards' magazines are empty, the camera will have done a 360-degree circle and will be facing the same way it started.

(206 words)

Screenplay

                    EXT. NEW YORK, 2025. DAY

The camera is following a helicopter flying over a mass of huge
skyscrapers. The camera passes over the top of the helicopter.
It then tilts 90 degrees downwards and drops down between the
skyscrapers. Before it hits the ground, the camera tilts up and
focuses on the entrance at the bottom of the skyscraper.

Police cars and vans are scattered around the base of the
skyscraper owned by the big businessmen identified by the
police as being behind the murders. The POLICE are well organised and there are lots of ARMED MEN waiting to go in and raid
the building. Some TV REPORTERS are trying to film the scene.
Among the police, there is a NINJA dressed in black with a
samurai sword.

Close-up of the CHIEF OF POLICE's face:

                    POLICE CHIEF
                (talking into his radio)

        We're going in!

The camera cuts to a medium shot from behind the NINJA,
showing her and a small force of armed POLICEMEN. The camera
then tracks sideways to the left.

A medium low level shot shows two groups of five POLICEMEN
with body armour and MP5 sub-machine guns. Both groups run to
the entrance of the skyscraper and kneel down, aiming their
guns at the window next to the door. The NINJA is standing
between the two groups.

The camera cuts to a 360-degree tracking shot, moving from
left to right, which circles the POLICE and the NINJA. The
group is then shot facing the skyscraper with their backs to
the camera. The POLICE fire at the glass. As they do, the
camera cuts to a medium long shot from inside the building,
looking out of the skyscraper. Glass shatters everywhere.

The next cut is to a tracking shot, next to the POLICE and the
NINJA, following them as they pick their way through the glass
into the building. They enter a big room with a high ceiling.
The room is constructed from two large hexagons, connected by a
short passageway filled with sophisticated security technology
(including metal detectors which we can see in the shot).

The audience sees the room from the point of view of three CCTV cameras located in the room. At the far end of the room is a row of ten lifts. Just after the POLICE enter the building, the lifts descend, the doors open and out of each lift steps an armed SECURITY GUARD. One of the guards is bigger than the rest: he is the CHIEF GUARD.

The next shot is a very fast tracking shot. Starting in the first hexagon, facing the lifts, it travels through the metal detectors and stops a couple of metres away from the CHIEF GUARD in the second hexagon. This cuts to a medium shot of the NINJA. She begins running and the camera tracks beside her. The camera is moving at a fractionally slower speed than the NINJA.

The camera then cuts to a POV shot from the NINJA's perspective. The NINJA and camera shoot forward.

Another cut back to the tracking shot beside the NINJA. It shows the NINJA jumping forward, through the metal detector, using her sword to deflect bullets that the CHIEF GUARD has shot at her. The NINJA slices the CHIEF GUARD.

A medium shot of the nine remaining GUARDS. Their faces are full of disbelief. They pull out their 9-mm Uzis and try to shoot the NINJA.

Cut to a long POV tracking shot, which begins next to the NINJA and follows the wall as she darts around the room avoiding bullets. Once all the GUARDS have emptied their clips, the POLICE run in and shoot the GUARDS.

The NINJA walks up to the chief guard, who is dying. The camera angle is a close-up from over the shoulder of the NINJA.

NINJA
(grabbing the guard)

What's the code for the lift?

Cut to a close-up of the NINJA, from behind the SECURITY GUARD.

NINJA
(forcefully)

If you don't tell me, I'll kill you.

```
                    CHIEF SECURITY GUARD
                    (panting and scared)

        Okay, Okay, I'll tell you. Just don't kill me
        — and protect me from 'them'.

    (breathing with difficulty, speaking slowly and quietly)

            The code is... 53872.
```

There is a cut to a close-up of the control panel for the lift. We see the NINJA's hand typing in the code. The camera cuts again to a medium long shot which shows the POLICE typing in the codes to the other lifts. Cut to a long shot which shows all of the lift doors open, the POLICE and the NINJA getting in and the lift doors closing.

Evaluation

The first shot tells the audience the location of the scene. When the camera drops down between the buildings, I intend it to concentrate the audience's attention. This signifies that the pace of the film is going to increase and that the climax of the film is coming up.

Many of the types of camera shot I use follow the conventions of the action genre. They have been used in other action films, such as *Spiderman* and *Lord of the Rings*. Halfway through the screenplay, when the police enter the building, the room is introduced to the audience via CCTV footage. This is important for two reasons. First, I think it is a fast way to introduce the audience to the complete layout of a room and, second, I think it is visually interesting. *The Matrix* includes a 360-degree action shot similar to the one I use in my screenplay. I want the action in my screenplay to be dynamic, unusual and contemporary. The influences for the storyline of my film include computer games, such as *Metal Gear Solid 2* and *Hitman 2*. Both these games include a genetically engineered man created to be a skilled fighter. I think there is a clear crossover between computer games and films in cinemas today and feel that this might add to potential audience interest.

The feedback I received for my screenplay was generally very positive. It was felt that the shots were easy to visualise. The screenplay was described as exciting and attention-grabbing. None of the people I received feedback from complained about the small amount of dialogue; they described it as appropriate within an action sequence.

Overall, I think that my screenplay is effective. It contains recognisable conventions of the action genre and has a comprehensible narrative movement. As well as attempting to create a believable sequence of events, I have tried to include shots that would be visually exciting for the audience.

(321 words)

🖉 An intriguing synopsis, which is convincing and typical of one type of action/thriller. The cinematic ideas are clear and original, showing a high level of understanding of film conventions and audience expectations. The screenplay more than fulfils the expectations created within the cinematic ideas. Details concerning camera setups and movements are particularly effective and appropriate to the genre of the film. There is plenty of visually exciting detail and the form of the piece is appropriate. The evaluation reports the success of the screenplay in communicating meaning through feedback from readers.

■ ■ ■

C-grade candidate's screenplay analysis of *The Reporter*

Synopsis

Amy Jackson, 24 years old, has taken 6 months off from her job as a news reporter to investigate the murder of her boyfriend, Gary Hobbes. She changes her image, style and clothing to undertake this report. With a new identity she looks and feels like a new person.

Amy (now known as Katy Wilson) goes undercover and gets a job working in the factory where Gary used to work. She suspects that his workmates had something to do with the murder. Richard Taylor, who works in the factory, becomes suspicious of Amy. They get to know each other very well and soon build up a strong relationship. Richard becomes involved in Amy's investigation and tries to help her.

With Richard's help, Amy has enough evidence to prove that Gary's workmates were involved in his killing. It turns out that Gary found out about a drugs scandal and that the manager of the factory, Paul Wade, who was involved in the drug selling, arranged for Gary to be killed. Richard and Amy make the front page of the local newspaper for being the town's heroes.

(183 words)

Cinematic ideas

The genre that my film follows is a thriller/romance. The sequence I have chosen is set early on in the film, where the audience needs to know who Gary was and how Richard and Amy become closer. My sequence should show the audience how Amy and Richard's relationship has become more trusting. The camerawork I will use to show this will include many close-ups to show the characters' expressions. This will make my sequence more realistic and natural. The long shots and medium shots will show the audience the settings and the characters' surroundings, which would add to the atmosphere. The lighting, when suspense is being built, should be quite dark, to show the audience that something bad is about to happen. In contrast, the lighting around Richard and Amy will be lighter, to show that they are the heroes of the film.

(145 words)

Screenplay

Amy	Hi, pleased to meet you.
Richard	Hi.

(They both look at each other, staring into each others' eyes, looking amazed. Medium shot of both of them and then close-ups of Richard and Amy's faces when they stare at each other.)

BLACKOUT.

Canteen

(Noisy atmosphere, with lots of people eating, drinking and talking. Extreme long shot of Amy walking towards the camera, with a lunch tray in her hand.)

Workmate	So what made you come and work in this dump?
Amy (shyly)	I fancied a change.

(The camera tracks her slowly as she sits down.)

Workmate	What do you think of it so far?
Amy	It's ok.
Workmate (sarcastically)	You're very chatty.

(They carry on eating their lunch. Amy is silent.)

Amy	Who is the man we met just then? The one in the green shirt?
Workmate	Richard. Why?
Amy	No reason.

(Cut to Amy sitting down, filling tubes with cream. She looks very bored. Richard taps her on the shoulder.)

Richard	Hi.
Amy	Oh, hello.
Richard	I was just wondering if you wanted to go for a coffee.
Amy (looking worried)	Sure. Why not?

(Cut to medium shot of the two having coffee.)

Richard	So, where do you come from?

Amy	The other side of London. You?

(An uneasy silence.)

Richard	Do your family live near here?
Amy	About half an hour away.
Richard	What made you come here then?
Amy	I fancied a change.
Richard (intrigued)	I can't imagine anybody thinking that this place was worth moving for.

(Amy looks nervous.)

Richard	Have you come on your own? Or with your boyfriend?
Amy (frustrated)	What makes you think I have a boyfriend?
Richard	No reason.

(Amy stands up abruptly and walks out of the canteen.)

(Cut to Amy sitting in her pyjamas, watching the television. There is a knock at the door. The camera follows Amy as she goes to open it.)

Amy (looking shocked)	Richard. What are you doing here? It's 11.30!
Richard	I'm sorry it's late. I just wanted to apologise for upsetting you today.
Amy	It's cold out there. You'd better come in.

(Cut to them both sitting down.)

Amy (tearful)	So when he died, I decided to take the investigation into my own hands. The police were useless.
Richard	God! Amy! I am so sorry.
Amy (yawning)	You didn't know.
Richard	Well. I'd better go. I'll see you at work tomorrow.

(Amy has fallen asleep. Richard covers her with a blanket and leaves. He leans over and kisses her on the cheek.)

BLACKOUT

Evaluation

This sequence aims to show how Amy and Richard's relationship builds without them even realising it. I have tried to do this by using close-ups and medium shots which place the couple together. I think that this works effectively. This sequence is created to show the romantic and soft side of the characters.

I received a lot of feedback on my screenplay. Many people said that they could understand that the relationship would develop in the later parts of the film. They said that the camerawork brought the characters closer and closer together. Some people also suggested that I could use a greater range of camerawork, in order to add interest for the viewer. One person who read the screenplay said that I could have added information about the characters' facial expressions, in order to give more information about their emotions to the viewer.

I hope that my sequence shows the difference in backgrounds between the two characters. By using micro elements such as cinematography and sound I feel that I have added atmosphere to the sequence. Overall, the feedback I received was positive, but I agree that I could have given more information about the characters' reactions through information about expressions.

(203 words)

The candidate's synopsis is clear and makes general narrative sense. The cinematic ideas are rather limited and focus mainly on cinematography. The points concerning camerawork detail intended meaning, but are somewhat basic. Other films of a similar genre or with similar cinematic ideas could have been used within this discussion. The screenplay creates realistic scenarios and does what it intends in terms of introducing the future relationship between the two protagonists. It includes some directorial detail, but needs far more in order to make the sequence come alive. The form of the screenplay is problematic and does not adhere to a conventional industry format. The evaluation is reflective and honest, but too short to gain a high mark.

Storyboard

A-grade candidate's storyboard analysis of *Sam's Children*

Synopsis

This is a story about a young man called Ben Phillips. The film follows his troubled life, after an honourable discharge from the US army during the Vietnam war. He is barely 23 when he arrives back to his first love and baby son.

The film opens with a scene of what appears to be Ben self-harming. We are soon made aware of why he does this, through a series of flashbacks to the horrific warfare in the Vietnam jungle. These flashbacks occur every day.

He decides that his only escape from the flashbacks is to go back to Vietnam and face his fears. When the armed forces refuse to reinstate him, he becomes even more detached and unstable. He loses his ability to distinguish between reality and fiction, and his flashbacks become even more severe.

His frustration and insanity finally take control during a particularly horrific flashback. He is gunned down in the street by police officers after brutally attacking a man after a trivial argument over a newspaper.

(170 words)

Cinematic ideas

I have chosen to do one of Ben's flashback sequences. To introduce Ben's flashback, I will use a quick cut to a close-up of his face after he has seen a picture in a magazine. This will make his face dominate the frame and indicate to the audience that he has seen something significant. We will then see a point-of-view shot of what he has seen.

There will then be a quick fade to white and a dissolve into his flashback. The sequence will then use a quick cut to a close-up of the face in the flashback, then a quick cut back to Ben's expression. The rapid transitions will give the impression that this is a very unnerving experience for Ben and one that he cannot control.

In shot 14 I will show an extreme close-up of Ben's face. His face will be to one side of the frame and in focus. His face then goes out of focus as the background moves into focus. In shot 13, I will use a low-angle shot to view Ben. I will also choose to use only non-diegetic sound to add to the impact of the scene.

Much of the scene has been influenced by Francis Ford Coppola's *Apocalypse Now**. This was a great influence, as my scene is also attempting to show the psychological damage of war on the film's protagonist.

(235 words)

Storyboard

SHOT I   DURATION: 8 SECONDS

FULL SHOT OF PROTAGONIST (BEN PHILLIPS)
CAMERA IS STATIC (CHARACTER DESCENDING STAIRS)
STRAIGHT CUT TO:

SHOT 2   DURATION: 6 SECONDS

MEDIUM SHOT OF BEN
DOLLY IN TO FACE (SLOWLY, 4 SECONDS)
DOLLY INTO:

SHOT 3   DURATION: 3 SECONDS

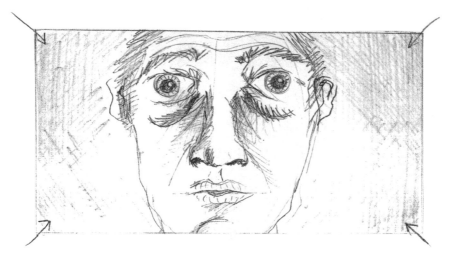

CU (CLOSE UP)
DIAGETIC SOUND: SHARP GASP
TO:

SHOT 4 STRAIGHT CUT   DURATION: 3 SECONDS

POV SHOT (POINT OF VIEW SHOT)

TO:

SHOT 5 FADE TO WHITE   DURATION: 0.25 SECONDS

DISSOLVE TO: MENTAL FLASHBACK

SHOT 6 POV SHOT (BEN'S)   DURATION: 0.50 SECONDS

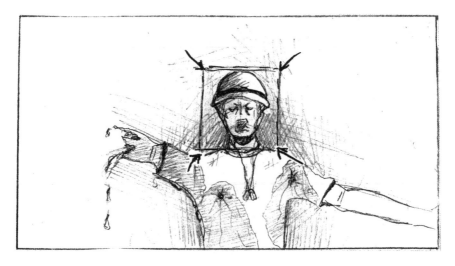

CUT TO SHOT 7:

SHOT 7 FACE IN FLASHBACK   DURATION: 1 SECOND

DIAGETIC SOUND: BLOODCURDLING SCREAM (NOT OF BEN)

CUT BACK TO: CLOSE UP OF BEN

SHOT 8   DURATION: 4 SECONDS

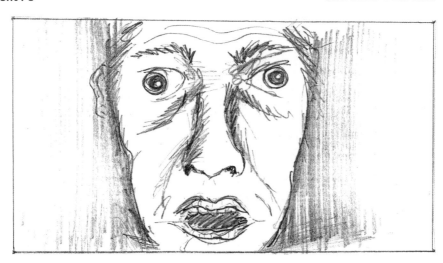

DIAGETIC SOUND: SCREAM FADES OUT

STRAIGHT CUT TO:

SHOT 9 MEDIUM CLOSE UP   DURATION: 1 SECOND

STRAIGHT CUT TO: WALL SHOT

SHOT 10   DURATION: 4 SECONDS

UNCLE SAM
NEEDS YOU!

POV SHOT
CAMERA MOVES FROM RIGHT TO LEFT (PANS ACROSS WALL)
WHEN WINDOW IS IN CENTRE OF FRAME DOLLY IN
DOLLY TO SHOT 11:

SHOT 11 CU OF SMASHED WINDOW   DURATION: 4 SECONDS

STRAIGHT CUT TO:

SHOT 12 CLOSE UP   DURATION: 1 SECOND

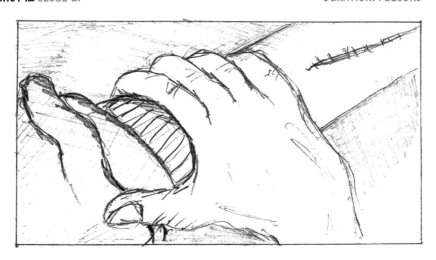

DISSOLVE TO SHOT 13:

SHOT 13 STATIC CAMERA MOVEMENT (NONE)　　　　　DURATION: 1.5 SECONDS

LOW ANGLE SHOT
DISSOLVE TO:

SHOT 14 ECU OF BEN IN FOCUS (BACKGROUND OUT OF FOCUS)　　　DURATION: 6 SECONDS

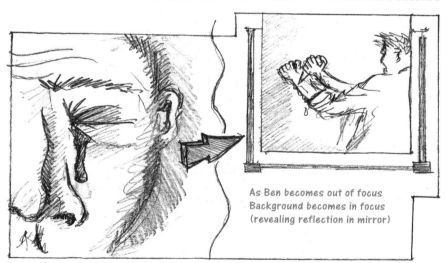

As Ben becomes out of focus
Background becomes in focus
(revealing reflection in mirror)

STRAIGHT CUT (SLOW MOTION) **TO:**

SHOT 15 CLOSE-UP OF GLASS   DURATION: 5 SECONDS

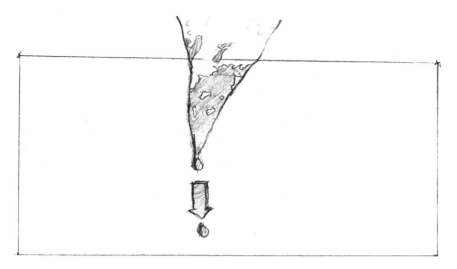

STRAIGHT CUT (SLOW MOTION) **TO:**

SHOT 16 ECU (EXTREME CLOSE UP)   DURATION: 4 SECONDS

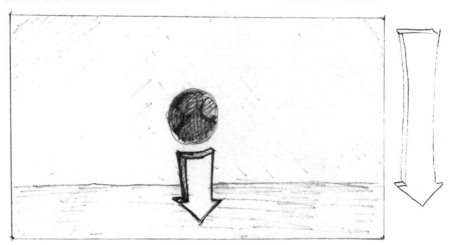

CAMERA TILT DOWNWARDS FOLLOWING BLOOD DROP

SHOT 17 CLOSE UP   DURATION: 2 SECONDS

TILT DOWN TILL IMPACT ON FLOOR
CUT TO:

SHOT 18 POV SHOT (POINT OF VIEW)   DURATION: 10 SECONDS

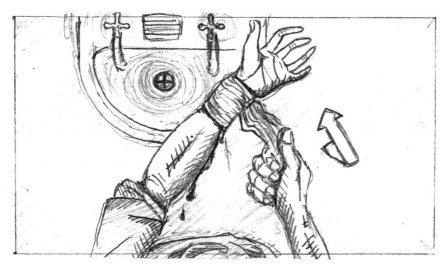

DISSOLVE TO SHOT 19:

SHOT 19 LONG SHOT   DURATION: 7 SECONDS

SHOT 20 FADE TO BLACK   DURATION: 3 SECONDS

Evaluation

As this is the opening sequence of my film, I wanted it to have a big impact on the viewer and to be a starting point for the viewer's understanding of the main character. Part of the feedback I received was that this sequence immediately immersed the viewer in the mind of the central character. In shots 1 and 2 I used a full shot, followed by a medium shot to show how alone and isolated the protagonist is. In shot 13, I used a low-angle shot to view Ben, which gives the audience the impression that he is unpredictable and maybe even dangerous. In shot 14, I have used an ECU of Ben's face, with his face to the left of the frame. As his face moves out of focus and the background becomes more prominent, a mirror image of him is revealed from behind. The switch in focus confuses the audience and adds to the sense of disorientation which the character feels.

The sequence builds up gradually, until the moment where we realise that he is self-harming. A very subtle realisation is achieved, by the shifts in focus within the scene. The audience gains understanding of Ben, but also a sense of sympathy towards him. The sequence also gives the audience a sense of what the rest of the film is going to be like. From the start, we are made subtly aware of his experiences in the army, from the objects on the walls and the flashback. The idea of psychological problems due to warfare is strongly associated with the war film genre and as a result gives the film a specific target audience.

Shots 15, 16 and 17 (where the blood is falling) were also commented on and seen as effective in the representation of Ben's plight. In my sequence, I decided to have very little sound. Feedback commented positively on this and it was suggested that the lack of sound added realism and impact to the scene. It is easier to focus on the protagonist when sound is minimal. I included the gasp to make the audience aware that the scene is very quiet and to indicate that we only hear what Ben does. Overall, I think my sequence produces the meanings I intended effectively.

(375 words)

🗎 The synopsis offers a tense and dramatic atmosphere for the film. The cinematic ideas are detailed and acknowledge their debt to an existing film text (*Apocalypse Now**). The storyboard sequence builds tension effectively and evidences a high level of knowledge of film conventions. A variety of well-framed and angled shots is used and detailed attention is paid to *mise-en-scène*. The presentation of the storyboard is effective and expresses complex ideas with clarity. The evaluation discusses intended meanings in detail and includes useful reference to actual responses. It is reflective and comprehensive.

■ ■ ■

C-grade candidate's storyboard analysis of *Ji*

Synopsis

Ten years ago, as part of a non-government-funded project, a group was formed, code-named Bourne. Its mission was to protect the world from terrorism. Soon afterwards, the group turned and became the most elite group of terrorists in the world. Our hero, Ji, was dropped from his high-ranking job when he uncovered the group's plan for world domination. After a trap laid by Kane, the leader of Bourne, Ji is caught and sent to prison for a crime he did not commit.

Present day: Ji is released from prison and is back with his love, Maria. She gives him the news that he is soon to be a father. Maria is kidnapped by Kane and Ji is forced to do some of his evil work. Kane also falls in love with Maria. With the help of some of his old colleagues, Ji discovers the place where Kane is holding Maria. There is a showdown in which Kane is killed and Ji triumphs. Ji's name is cleared and he and Maria look forward to the birth of their child.

(182 words)

Cinematic ideas

My inspiration for the storyboard came from *Metal Gear Solid* (Konami, 2000), a video game. The sequence I have chosen takes place near the conclusion of my film, where Ji makes a final assault on his enemy Kane. My inspiration from *Metal Gear Solid* can be seen in shots of Ji close up against a wall when he is hiding from the guard. He is shot at a low angle. This is similar to techniques used in the video game.

I also took inspiration from the film *The Rock* (Michael Bay, 1999), particularly the section where they infiltrate Alcatraz prison. I hope to use the same dark lighting that they used in the scenes there. The dark lighting will help to generate the effect of the unknown. I also wish for special effects to be used in part of my sequence. When Ji discovers the trap, he lights a cigarette and, at this point, I would like the lasers to become visible. I also wish for there to be no music at the beginning of my sequence, as this will help build suspense.

(181 words)

Storyboard

SHOT 1 MS Dark lighting showing Ji pressed up against a wall with a guard oblivious to what's going on

SHOT 2 Close-up

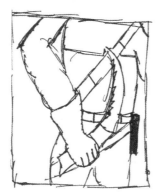

SHOT 3 MS Still shot showing Ji killing guard

FADE TO BLACK

SHOT 4 MS Slow tracking shot from left to right until it reaches open door

CUT TO

SHOT 5 CU Bomb slowly ticking

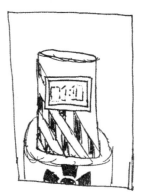

SHOT 6 LS Maria tied up around the bomb. Dark lighting apart from computer screen.

SHOT 7 Camera shot from Ji's gun pointed directly at Maria

SHOT 8 CU Cut to Maria talking to Ji

SHOT 9 LS CCTV shot zooming into where infrared sensors are

SHOT 10 CU on Ji's face. Room fills with smoke.

SHOT 11 MS As the room fills with smoke infrared sensor becomes clear

SHOT 12 LS of Ji moving around lasers

SHOT 13 MCU taken from laser of Ji moving around laser

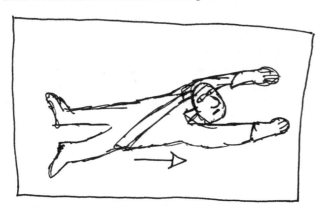

SHOT 14 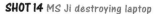 MS Ji destroying laptop

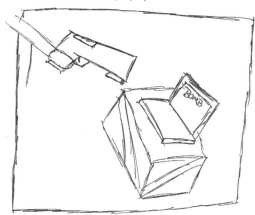

Evaluation

When I reflect on what I produced, I think that the effects I wanted to get across were clear. My personal favourites are the first three shots of my sequence. I think the sequence I have created goes well with the film as a whole. There were some uncertainties, however, when I showed my storyboard to people in my target group. I think this is down to my drawing skills and the way the piece was edited. I think the pace of the piece was possibly too fast for the audience.

There are many shots I am pleased with, in particular the first person shot from Ji's gun. I think the right atmosphere was created by my shots, like the first one taken from a low angle in order to show the situation the character was in. There were some readings of the film which I did not intend. Some people thought that Maria was dead and hanging from the chains. I'll put that down to my drawing skills. The intended meaning was that she was tied to the chains, waiting to be rescued by Ji. I think that one of the shots which could have been improved was the one of Ji lighting a cigarette. I think that this could have been done more powerfully; however, I do like the fact that the identity of the character is not revealed until the end of the film. I think that this adds mystery.

I feel that I could have added another shot to help the narrative structure, as people did not understand why the laptop was shot immediately. I feel that if I had added a shot from behind the laptop, proving that it was not plugged in, then this might have helped. I think that the laptop was essential to my *mise-en-scène*, as the light coming from it invited the audience to look closer. Overall, I am pleased with my storyboard and in particular with the atmosphere it generates, but feel that I could have improved the sense of the narrative.

(344 words)

🖉 The synopsis is clear and convincingly typical of an action thriller. There is some consideration of intended formal elements within the cinematic ideas, but these are not developed fully. A statement about intended audience is needed. The storyboard